Lightning In a Bottle:

A Book Series On the Most Important Rock Albums In Music History

Album #69

Frank Zappa

Hot Rats

To view all of Charlie Freak's books available for sale in this book series on the Most Important Rock Albums in Music History, visit his Author's Page at lulu.com,

http://www.lulu.com/spotlight/charliefreak1

Or, visit Charlie Freak's website at,

https://charliefreak1.wixsite.com/website

All proceeds from the sale of these books go to the Casa Lothlorien Animal Rescue Shelter here in Mexico.

Author, Charlie Freak and his posse...

Lightning In a Bottle:

A Book Series On the Most Important Rock Albums In Music History

<u>Album #69</u>

Frank Zappa

Hot Rats

by Charlie Freak

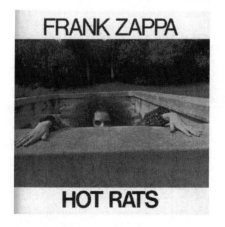

COPYRIGHT PAGE

LIGHTNING IN A BOTTLE:
A Book Series On the Most Important Rock Albums In Music History
ALBUM #69
Frank Zappa
Hot Rats

I am neither a lawyer, nor a licensed health care practitioner. This book series, website and the content provided herein are simply for educational purposes and do not take the place of your own common sense, legal advice from your attorney and/or medical information from your personal caretaker. The information and beliefs expressed within this book series represent the author alone, and are not meant to replace your own exhaustive treatments of the various subjects. No liability is assumed for losses or damages due to the information provided. You are responsible for your own choices, actions, and results. You should consult your attorney for your own specific publishing and disclaimer questions and needs. Thank you.

TABLE OF CONTENTS

Foreword..6

Dedications..71

Album Information....................................72

Album Cover/Art Design........................75

Album Overview.....................................79

Track 1 - Peaches en Regalia................98

Track 2 - Willie the Pimp.....................109

Track 3 - Son of Mr. Green Genes........128

Track 4 - Little Umbrellas.....................136

Track 5 - The Gumbo Variations..........151

Track 6 - It Must Be a Camel................162

Epilogue...175

FOREWORD

To see the full list of the 150 Most Important Rock Albums in Music History, it is found on pages 64-69, at the end of this Foreword...thank you.

First, let me personally thank you for purchasing this book. I can assure you that you will, at the very least, find all of the books in this series very entertaining and topical! Topical because the information and messages that the artists who created these sonic masterpieces provided us with were honest, integral and truthful...and in a world that has become built upon Lies and is completely upside down (and I mean this LITERALLY) this makes these albums not only vitally important, but "au courant" as well!

Nine years ago, my wife and best friend, Colleen, sat me down to watch a documentary entitled, Zeitgeist, by Peter Joseph. It was an experience that neither of us will ever forget. Both of us had spent our lives outside of societal norms, and did things quite differently from most of society (we both enjoy an active lifestyle, with a Vegetarian diet, we didn't vaccinate our youngest child, Spencer, we always tried to do things for our selves before consulting help from others, our doctor was a Naturopathic physician, not an M.D., and we read a lot of books, listened to a lot of music but rarely watched mainstream television or movies). Thus, we have always been different from the status quo, preferring to do things our own way. However, after watching the Zeitgeist documentary, we went much further "down the rabbit hole" than we even knew was possible. Shortly after this, we watched the Matrix movie series, all three parts, the academy-award winning movie, Network and the animal cruelty documentary, Food Inc. Wow, our paradigm had shifted, once again, dramatically into a whole other realm of Truth! And within a couple of years from this experience we decided, without much of a plan, to sell all of our possessions and investments in Canada, and move to the year-round warmth and relative unknown of Mexico!

It has been quite the journey, with many an unexpected turn along the way, however, neither of us would change a thing. We purposefully turned away from an organized society in Canada that was founded upon white lies, massive taxes, the institutionalized raising and slaughtering of innocent animals, and a political system that was "only in it for the money"; to a reality where we are essentially free and truly responsible for ourselves! Our home, Casa Lothlorien, is in the Mexican countryside, in a mountainous valley south of

Cuernavaca, Morelos, Mexico. We have a large home on a large piece of land, without neighbors, and are surrounded by agrarian fields in production (Sugar Cane, Corn and Soya)...we also have free-grazing Cattle and Horses roaming all around us (along with large spiders and scorpions!). We, quite naturally, responded to a problem in the area of many injured or stray animals. Thus, we have created the Casa Lothlorien Animal Rescue Sanctuary! When we encounter lost or injured animals we bring them into our home and take care of them. If we are able to find excellent homes for them, we will allow people to adopt our animals; however, if there aren't any qualified homes, then they become part of our large, extended family. Right now, Colleen and I have 20 dogs, 3 cats, 4 birds, 2 horses and a goat...to us, they are not merely animals, they are truly members of our family!

Now, all of the infrastructure that we have acquired or built for our rescued animals, and all of the food, supplies and medicine that they need requires a sizeable amount of funds. So, Colleen came up with the idea for me to write this book series and have the proceeds from the sale of the books to go towards our costs for running this program. Thus, when you purchase one of our books, not only are you receiving a wonderfully honest and entertaining source of information, but you are supporting a great cause! So, we do truly thank you, from the bottom of our hearts, for your Love and Support of our entire Family! An average day here in Mexico for Colleen and I, involves taking care of our home, our animals and ourselves. Typically, after our chores are done, and we have had breakfast, Colleen and I will play a game together (where we create our own rules), and then we move on to our "work"...Colleen is a brilliant artist and in her art room she creates amazing pieces of art that simply astound me! While I retreat to my office, overlooking all the fields of Sugar Cane, with all the dogs and cats around me, and I sit down and write...and write...and write! For seven years I wrote, almost non-stop to create this book series, entitled, Lightning in a Bottle: The Most Important Rock Albums in Music History. I have now completed all 150 books in this series on the 150 most important albums, and I am now, along with Colleen's help, releasing all of them for sale in both Print and Ebook formats for everyone to purchase at Lulu.com! We chose to sell our books on Lulu.com because they actually have the audacity to care for people, including Authors foolish enough to self-publish their work! And we bless them for all their help and beautifully kind words of support! So, what gives me the right to undertake this massive book series on something as personal and complex as Rock and Roll albums you ask, with all this discussion about Truth, Honesty,

Integrity and Personal
Excellence??? Well, let's discuss
that a little...

"We now live in a nation where doctors
destroy health, lawyers destroy justice,
universities destroy knowledge, governments
destroy freedom, the press destroys
information, religion destroys morals, and our
banks destroy the economy."
~ Chris Hedges ~

My life, in many aspects, has been a
love affair with music, both playing it
and and listening to it. I spent my
own money as a young man to take
piano lessons through the music
conservatory, just to be able to play
the music that I was listening
to...songs that connected to my heart
in ways that I didn't fully understand,
yet I knew there was a powerful
connection and bond. So many of
the songs that I heard when I began
listening to music literally hit me like
thunderbolts (lightning)...I was so
moved by their powerful sonic

landscapes. Thus, as a young man, I began a MASSIVE album collection that really defined so much of my personal journey. These artists and albums that I gravitated to became the soundtrack for my life, and when I "look back" on events in my life, I find that they are ALL connected to a specific album or song! In other words, I don't really have any sense of "time" from my memories, rather simply connections to the music that I was absorbed with when these events took place...now that's pretty cool! When I began to put together "bands" to play smaller gigs for events and parties, invariably the set lists were filled with the songs of these artists that I loved, creating some of the most BIZARRE playlists that I think that anyone had ever put together. I remember one band in particular that I created and played in, Creatures From the Black Lagoon (some of my other band names included, The Leather Canaries, The Deflatable Tomatoes and Hell's Angels Eat Quiche), a 4-piece group

13

of high school students and we
played each Thursday night at the
local University's Sub-Pub (Student
Union Building) where, to get the gig,
I had to agree to do a lot of the
"music of the day", which in those
days was Punk, New Wave and Top
40. However, I was really into the
Classics from the Fifties and the
Sixties, as well as Zappa and Steely
Dan. Thus, some of the song
combinations were stunningly
bizarre...and because this particular
band wasn't that great, everything
tended to sound the same, so a lot of
the Punk and New Wave songs
began to take on psychedelic
overtones...which made for some
interesting sets!!!

As I grew from my teenage years in
the Seventies and the mid-Eighties,
into my "adult" life into the Nineties, I
found that work and social
engagements were constantly
putting me at odds with my music.
And that the further I expanded into
these societal roles the less time I

had for music, and the less happy I found myself becoming. The Music Industry's decision to change the format for music from the richness and warmth of Analogue LPs to the cold, calculating, void of Digital CDs only furthered my sense of disconnection from Music. It was clear to even the most non-discerning eye, that by the Nineties the Music Industry had changed forever and it was never going back to the "heyday" of Rock and Roll. Gone were all the Classic artists and bands, replaced by a plethora of new artists who lacked many things, but one component in particular, and that was Heart! Essentially, from the mid-Eighties onward, popular music was hijacked by the Record Industry to take away creativity, non-conformity, the cutting-edge and genius, and replace them with conformist banality...MEDIOCRITY! Suddenly, all the music that was being played publically (within the Mainstream) all sounded the same, and was being written and performed without PASSION! And let's be honest, the central founding tenets of Rock and Roll were Passion, Intensity, Honesty and Non Conformity! Chuck Berry wasn't writing about consuming worthless consumer products, just so that he could fit in and conform to societal norms, he was OUTRAGEOUSLY attacking the very system that was crushing honesty, integrity, individuality and excellence! Buddy Holly, in a very short period of time, went from pioneering a new age of Pop music that observed aspects of society, passively, to aggressively writing an entirely new genre of music that pushed the boundaries of societal norms for something more...something better. Bob Dylan went from becoming a "one-trick pony" protesting about every injustice that came along, to subversively turning society upside down by writing cleverly structured songs that unveiled what society actually was...all without letting the

listener know that this was what he
was doing!

Chuck Berry was singing that "Beethoven" to
me...

Buddy Holly saw possibilities in Rock Music
that most couldn't even conceive of...

Dylan learned that you could shoot a
"bazooka" full of Truth out loud, as long as it
was disguised with a little musical "honey"

However, the roots of Rock and Roll
truly reside within two unique
aspects of American society. One,
was the musical troubadour, touring
around the countryside, from town-
to-town, hopping freight-cars, cross-
tie walking, sharing their wisdom and
songs for food and lodgings, all the
while LISTENING to what was going
on in the lives of everyday
Americana...hearing the TRUTH and
REALITY of what was really
happening within the microcosm of

the world, instead of via the "news" of the macrocosm. Woody Guthrie was the very finest example of these men and women who were simply "made of music" and lived their lives this way. So the folk sound and heritage of grassroots honesty and truth telling in Rock and Roll comes from this wonderful tradition of the troubadours. The second basis for Rock music was the Blues, in particular the authentic Mississippi River/Delta Blues, meaning those Black men and yes, even some women, that suffered the most racial abuse and capitalistic exploitation that perhaps ANY one group of people have ever suffered on our Earth. Their release of this pain was a special kind of music where the listener could feel the suffering both in the sound of the acoustic guitar and in the delivery of the words...this was a cathartic experience as they were letting go of all their pain in the moment, knowing full well that when the song was over, they were going right back into sorrow and torment (even more so psychological than physical). Therefore, the Blues was aptly named and its legacy of hurt, pain, anguish, and of course, speaking one's personal TRUTH was also etched into the foundations of Rock and Roll through the voice of the disenfranchised! Thus, Rock and Roll music was created through the RAW PASSION of men and women who feared that they would never be truly free without the "comfort" of death. It is this metal, forged within these two fires, that resulted in this musical tour de force...and to see what it has become today is nothing short of a physical crime!

Modern music is people who can't think signing artists who can't write songs to make records for people who can't hear.

— Frank Zappa —

All that is heard, for free, on the radio or video stations anymore is the "Top Forty", and this kind of music has NEVER promoted creativity, individuality, honesty, integrity or personal excellence; rather only the Corporate axiom of consume more and think less!

And then, approximately eight years ago, I watched a program via the internet on the "State of the Music Industry", and the person being interviewed stated that it was the first year (since records had been kept on album sales) that not one single album within Popular music was going to reach one million in sales (which floored me, thinking of Pink Floyd's, The Wall, selling north of 25 million copies, or Michael Jackson's Thriller selling north of 100 million copies); plus, he alleged that this apathy towards buying albums from the public (of which some of it was due to piracy), was purposeful, designed by the record industry itself to kill off the album as an art form, and replace it with singles and music videos. Why? The answer lay in all other aspects of society, especially within youth culture, where all seemed to possess the attention spans of gnats. It was clear that everywhere one turned, society was purposefully turning human minds from deep reflectors and critical thinkers into mindless zombies only concerned with what was going on right in front of them, right now. And if anyone took the time to stand back for a moment and observe what societal youth had in front of them in any moment, it was some kind of electronic gadget with an "App", something to distract the mind away from things that mattered, into ridiculous forms of materialism and Pop Culture that didn't matter at all! And this is why I have taken the last seven years of my life, day-after-day, to write this book series. To stand up for what is right about humanity, which is the human being (the free-thinking individual who rarely follows what others do, instead preferring to follow their own path). To powerfully say NO to distractions, lazy minds, ambivalence and MEDIOCRITY and say YES to caring, to focus, to passion to PERSONAL EXCELLENCE! To celebrate the truthful origins of Rock and Roll and all that it has meant to the people of the world. To celebrate the Rock Album as an incredibly important art form and source of truth...this wondrous artistic creation where personal messages were alive and abundant...where auditory and graphic art were brought together with the most sublime results. To celebrate the essence of Truth, Love and Integrity that is God. To resurrect that which is sacred about real music and to remind everyone of what has been taken from us, by force! Thus, this book series on the Most Important Albums in Music History is about far more than "just some Rock songs", it's about the struggle for human survival as passionate, loving, caring, focused individuals who exist to follow their own stars to the best of their own abilities! To become their own SHINNING STARS who cast their own unique light of genius upon the rest of us, as part of a humanity that is humble before God and Mother Nature and passionate about sharing, loving and giving unto others...

"When any government, or any church for that matter, undertakes to say to its subjects, 'This you may not read, this you must not see, this you are forbidden to know,' the end result is tyranny and oppression, no matter how holy the motives. Mighty little force is needed to control a man whose mind has been hoodwinked; contrariwise, no amount of force can control a free man, a man whose mind is free. No, not the rack, not fission bombs, not anything—you can't conquer a free man; the most you can do is kill him."
Robert A. Heinlein, If This Goes On, 1940

Okay, so if all of this is true, then how did the art form, known as Rock and Roll music, become a hollow shell by 1984 (what an appropriate year)? How did the very nature of Rock become the ANTITHESIS of what it was founded upon and what it stood for? The fact is, Rock and Roll music exists in two very powerful realities, one is the art form, innocent and pure, while the other is the ASSET...something of value that can be OWNED (often by little white men, hiding behind curtains); thus, capable of being shaped and manipulated...CONTROLLED. When I was young, my innocence and naiveté only allowed me to see and hear the brilliance of Music as an art form and overlook its business reality. However, as I grew into yet another work and debt slave, toiling away at a "job" that I didn't like, I became aware of Music as an Industry, controlled and manipulated by "someone". The question, for me, became, "who was the someone?" And the answer that I discovered through all of my research was that a small group of occultist elitists, who hoard all assets, make up the Music Industry, centered in Century City, California, just a hop, skip and jump from Beverly Hills and Hollywood...no coincidence there...

Century City DID NOT EXIST prior to the invention of Rock and Roll as an "own-able asset", it was CREATED with forethought and malice by those who wished to market and own the musical art form known as Rock and Roll. And if you have never visited Century City, it is a site to be seen, and then quickly forgotten. It is a 176-acre CONCRETE JUNGLE filled with record industry Executives, Lawyers and "hitmen", the guys who deliver messages, get contracts signed and say "hello" once and awhile to the artists...

From the sky you can see just how small this
neighborhood of Los Angeles is, and the only
greenery that exists is that of the two small
condo developments for the vastly wealthy
who reside in Century City, part-time.

Century City represents the
wealthiest neighborhood in all of Los
Angeles (and one of the wealthiest in
the world), it also possesses an
almost ALL-WHITE population
(almost 90%); however, most of
these white people in Century City
were not born in America, and
interestingly enough, most of these
hold dual citizenship between the
United States and Israel...hmmm.
You see, we tend to think of the
music industry as a happenstance, a
necessary attempt to divine order out

27

of the chaos that was the innocent and miraculous invention of Rock and Roll...its NOT! The Music Industry is a FORCE, a giant Corporation that holds hundreds of smaller corporations within it, all subservient to the head of the snake! And as with all legal Corporations within the United States, the number one tenet, or Law, is to MAXIMIZE PROFIT! Any Corporate Head, or Board, found guilty of dismissing this single tenet can be removed by the shareholders for their sins...

"Or bring me a girl they're always the best
You put 'em on stage and ya' have 'em
undress
Some angel whore who can learn a guitar lick
Hey, now that's what I call music"

From the Tom Petty song, Joe, from the
album, The Last DJ

Therefore, when we think of the
music of Rock and Roll, we simply
can no longer hold onto these puppy
dog, sentimental images of Elvis and
Fats Domino encouraging us to get
off the sofa and shake our hips.

Rock and Roll is a CONSTRUCT, just like Television and Movies are constructs...they are all own-able assets that serve valuable purposes for their Corporate Masters; and as such, virtually no-one and nothing is left "to chance" within these industries...including their "Stars" who create, sing, and/or act their product!!! This is why brilliant writers and researchers such as Dave McGowan (Weird Scenes Inside the Canyon: Laurel Canyon, Covert Ops and the Dark Heart of the Hippie Dream) and Mark Devlin (Musical Truth: Volumes 1 and 2) have been able to detect the same "fingerprints" and DNA of the controllers of society to the backgrounds of the artists who make Rock and Roll music and act on TV and in the movies...

Lookout Mountain Laboratory

What did all these musicians have in common with wannabe musician, Charles Manson, and why were they all conveniently located living within the confines of Laurel Canyon and its "out of the way" location? And why was this facility (to the right), the CIA's Lookout Mountain Laboratory, located at the top of the hill in Laurel Canyon? Why did Frank Zappa believe (living in the famous "Log Cabin" in Laurel Canyon) that the "dazed and confused" fellow who paid him a visit one day with a gun and orders to kill him, was from the CIA??? So many questions and so few answers...

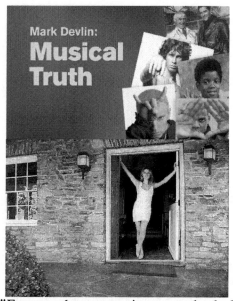

"Everyone there at one time or another had been into Satanism, or, like myself, had dabbled around the edges for sexual kicks." Sammy Davis Jr.
Part of the Music Industry's "Rat Pack", on the Manson Family murder victims located at 10050 Cielo Drive, the home of Roman Polanski and his then 'girlfriend', Sharon Tate (top right).

How did Jim Morrison, of the Doors (bottom left) go from visiting his Father, George Stephen Morrison, U.S Navy Rear Admiral, on the deck of his US Naval Aircraft Carrier (top left) to Rock and Roll icon (right) in a matter of only 4 short years??? And why was his father the Commander of the U.S. naval forces in the Gulf of Tonkin during the Gulf of Tonkin Incident of August 1964, which has now been proved, beyond a shadow of doubt, NEVER EVEN OCCURRED??? Just another governmental FALSE FLAG event!

However, this next point is one that is extremely important to discuss and understand...Rock and Roll grew faster than even the controllers of society could have imagined! Building off the mania of Elvis and his many contemporaries in the Fifties and early Sixties, the music industry was exploding into hundreds of millions of homes across this Earth; thus, the industry needed an ever-growing list of artists...and for a short period of time, they opened the proverbial flood gates and a number of brilliant and AUTHENTIC musicians snuck through. Honest, integral people who not only wanted the ability to create their own music, but to share their questions and ideas with everyone else...a perfectly HUMAN thing to do. Literally, thousands of these musicians were allowed in "behind enemy lines", and thus, a war to regain control of the music industry began almost immediately...a battle that lasted almost 15 years! So, you might be asking yourselves, if the music industry is so well-structured and controlling as I have alleged, then how did they ever make this "mistake" in the first place? Because, as I laid out for you, the industry needed the Supply to match the massive Demand that was exploding for Rock and Roll, everywhere. The powers that be, had no idea that Rock and Roll (rebellion) would grab ahold of the masses as quickly and as deeply as it did. So, to fill their "quotas", they opened up their doors to just about everyone (even Charlie Manson was on the outskirts). But, the industry still felt that they would be able to control all of these "newcomers" through the wonderfully insane world of Record Contracts. As most of you know, the initial recording contract for virtually every artist is both figuratively and literally a swindle. Most of these kids that answered "the call" to become Rock stars in the Sixties were wide-eyed idealists and artists...they did NOT possess business acumens...and as such they were taken for big ol' rides!

I could write an entire book just listing out the absolute worst record contracts in music history (CCR with Fantasy Records), there are so many. Suffice-it-to-say, these contracts were not the exception, they were the norm! And most of the comments from judges, ruling on contract disputes between artists and labels over the years, have been rooted in medieval language. As such, many of the artists who had the money and the courage to take their labels to court over these unconscionable contracts WON a form of freedom and independence from their labels (two of the best examples were Frank Zappa and Tom Petty). However, MOST did not fight their labels; most "played along" with their first contracts the best they could (often ending up massively in DEBT), and then "made it big" as "free agents" with their second contracts...you know, the price of doing business in Century City with the Devil. Just ask either John Fogerty or Tom Petty (in your prayers) how well things went in both their professional AND personal lives after targeting the music industry? Tom Petty had his well-secured home burnt to a crisp by what investigators labelled as "professional arsonists", and not some whack-job with three names loitering about a la Mark David Chapman or Lee Harvey Oswald! Thus, these contracts were PURPOSEFUL! They were designed for one reason, and it wasn't "just for the money"; these contracts were constructed this way to CONTROL human beings...and did they ever work!

"Having read JFK and the Unspeakable (James W. Douglass' stunning novel) several years ago, I've been thinking about assassinations for quite a while and I've seen how 'conspiracy theory' is used to shut off debate, to signal that we're entering 'the unspeakable' zone. So I began to wonder if the use of the term Conspiracy Theory might be a conspiracy itself. So I went exploring, and surprise surprise, there is a 1967 CIA memo that puts forward a great many of the commonly heard rebuttals to the Warren Commission Report. The CIA owned over 250 media outlets in the 1960s, spent close to a billion dollars (in today's dollars) spreading information, and had people doing its bidding in every major city in the world, so it is not surprising that they were able to disseminate this idea. And the issue is contemporary, too, not just historical. Cass Sunstein is a powerful Obama Administration insider whose new book, Conspiracy Theories and Other Dangerous Ideas, is a sophisticated apology for the established order.

Rev. Douglas Wilson, member of the Core Group of Project Unspeakable

Now, I am sharing all of this with you because of the consequences these artists had to deal with after signing contracts such as these with Century City. Anyone who thinks that the music industry is "fine" with their stable of artists giving away their secrets as to who is behind all of the corruption in the world, is simply fooling themselves. There have always been "prices to pay" for artists attempting to spread any form of the truth to the masses. As such, ALL ARTISTS that do business with Century City or Hollywood feel pressure! And for a long, LONG time these artists have learned to couch their words/messages behind complexity, ambiguity and multiple layers of meanings. Just think of the best musical example of all time...Bob Dylan. While Dylan was playing the role as the "angry young man", writing one straight-forward protest song after another, he was the relatively unknown, but talented performer from Minnesota. But once Dylan became the LSD-tripping poet travelling across America on, Another Side of Bob Dylan, he instantly became the genius "singer-songwriter" from Columbia records who was recommending "tripping on acid" to anyone who would listen. After this, coincidentally, Dylan's brilliant songs began to be covered by Columbia Record's most POPULAR artists, and this catapulted Dylan's professional career to a whole other level. Now, let me be clear, Dylan is the "real deal" when it comes to music and his lyrics...there's Dylan and then there's everyone else in many aspects of songwriting. But there's a reason why Dylan gave that cryptic interview with 60 Minutes back in 2004...

https://youtu.be/m_wAZ02JUtM

Dylan did indeed make a deal with the devil, as he shared with millions of viewers on television..."with the chief commander...on this Earth and in the world we can't see." A deal that saw Dylan obscure his allegorical lyrics with complexities and in riddles that made the truth difficult for the "passer-by" to clearly see. Plus, Dylan agreed to begin promoting the use of the CIA's weaponized drug, LSD; and in doing so, like a Pied Piper of sorts, he led many of his followers down a path of distraction and uncertainty. Dylan pioneered this new wave of songwriting though the Sixties and the Seventies where it became possible to interpret an artist's words 101 different ways. This is now often referred to as, what Professor Tolkien coined, "applicability". The artist's ability to camouflage direct meanings or comparisons (allegories) to their words. Dylan, like Tolkien, did this to be able to get his work released to widespread, mainstream audiences. Regardless of what Professor Tolkien wrote at the beginning of the Lord of the Rings, you absolutely CAN make direct (one-to-one) comparisons from his book to the "real" world...but not in the way(s) that most would imagine. Thus, enter my services and the importance of this book series. My unique ability to see and understand these songwriters, and the absolute heart of their messages, has become very necessary in this day and age because the artistic "messages" of this world have now become complex and convoluted...open to endless speculations; instead of simple interpretations to simple truths! This is now our sad reality...that the best, most important albums of all time are hidden behind self-imposed protections, to some extent, and that their integral, important messages are not "plain to see" for the masses! To many people, these albums are simply complex riddles that "sound good"; therefore, my task, in this mammoth book series, is to UNVEIL TRUTHS, something that these artists simply wouldn't or believed they couldn't do. To unveil the core messages to these songs and the larger themes of these albums.

"The way that I write allows a lot of people to interpret in their own fashion. I am not just saying one thing. I am saying a lot of things to a lot of people. The music means different things to different people. I want to insist that every listener makes a tiny bit of effort to reach the music and interpret what I am saying. My words put out feelers. It's up to listeners to pick up on them and get from them what they wish - I'm not attempting to be clear-cut. I want to deal in terms that invite questioning. Balm for the masses is no use whatsoever. We do tend to judge music on its rhythms and whether you can tap your foot to it. But most of our music deserves to be listened to several times. I'm still listening to Beethoven and I still don't understand what he is doing, but I'll get there some day. God knows that whatever I ultimately make of Beethoven I will never derive the same interpretation as what was intended - and I hope he respects my right to my interpretation - but at least I have a willingness to try to understand it. I don't really want to get into specific comparisons and explanations, especially about Passion Play and Thick As A Brick. I don't want to start people off trying to figure out where the new album is in relation to the last two. Believe it or not, they all mean something. It's distinctly worrying, because I know that the last few records have been difficult to listen to. War Child, so I'm told, is a lot more accessible. I don't know if I like that or not. I've started to worry that perhaps

Not all artists wrote with applicability
as a forced measure...some, such as
the aforementioned Dylan, Jethro
Tull (above), Steely Dan and Joni
Mitchell did so as an art form; and
thus, differed greatly from the
directness of say Neil Young,
George Harrison, Roger Hodgson
and Joe Strummer. The
aforementioned artists preferred to
write their lyrics with applicability,
and thus, make their songs as open
to interpretation as possible to allow
the listener to "grow" in their
understanding of these songs. For
some, Steely Dan's, Josie, is an
upbeat song about the old
neighborhood getting excited for the
return of their favorite
daughter...having fun for a weekend,
living it up, breaking a few rules;

however, to others, Josie is the epitome of anarchy and the need for organized society to collapse...a song as subversive as anything ever written...the choice is up to the listener and their own experiences. While the principle messages of Neil Young's Ohio or Roger Hodgson's School cannot be missed by even the casual listener. Each style has its own merit and value; however, MOST Rock and Roll songs, since the mid-Sixties, have taken on dual meanings, if not endless layers of possible interpretations. And I am NOT anti-applicability; there are tremendous gifts to be received by listeners being forced to dig deeper into the hidden meanings within songs; however, not all artists and not all songs need to be couched in riddles! There is too much applicability in modern art, in my opinion, and not enough direct communication...and it is my central thesis that the reason for this is conspiratorial in nature...that artists (for a long time) have been coerced through education, monetary incentives and threatening means to obscure the central truths in their messages. Thus, entire catalogues for bands like the Alan Parsons Project have been written-off, over time, as passive and unimportant in nature, rather than as absolutely integral! Eric Woolfson and Alan Parsons did such an amazing job of layering the various meanings within their lyrics that for most people their stunning album, Turn of a Friendly Card, is a simple, direct allegory against the "demons" of gambling; and thus, not really to be considered as an "important" Rock album. Just more "boring" office music from two middle-aged perfectionists, right? WRONG! Turn of a Friendly Card is a creative, vibrant and powerful sermon as to how the world is run; and why most people function as ignorant slaves, blindly supporting the very system that incarcerates their hopes and dreams! The Turn of a Friendly Card musical suite on side two is as IMPORTANT a piece of music as you will ever listen to (not to mention beautiful and moving). Thus, the entire Rock and Roll industry has become muddled, disjointed and misjudged (ON PURPOSE), as Rock Critics uniformly encourage all listeners to "rush to judgment" on all albums; instead of patiently waiting for the songs to slowly open and reveal themselves, as many bottles of superior red wine do, almost magically, when you give them the necessary time! Steely Dan's album, Gaucho, was mindlessly VILIFIED at the time of its release by critics as being the height of self-indulgence and tedious Rock music; however, every year since, as the subversive masterpiece it is, the album has continued to release more and more of its varied "fragrances", slowly revealing itself to be one of the best and most important Rock albums, EVER!

So, why? Why do Rock and Roll music critics rush off and label artists and albums as one thing, only to REWRITE HISTORY with REVISIONIST reviews a decade later? Why create these transparent and pathetic attempts at salvaging their integrities and reputations??? Because MOST (not all) critics write for institutions that are in place to HELP the Music Industry maintain their control over artists and the mainstream beliefs of the record-buying public. They are all part of ONE big, miserable family that controls society. Thus, what most people believe about Rock songs, bands, and Rock and Roll in general, is whatever the music industry WANTS US TO BELIEVE! Just ask Pete Townshend or Roger Waters how accurate the various Rolling Stone album reviews have been over the years about their band's albums!!! This is society's number one trick...rush to judgment! Just as Mark Lane wrote about in 1964 regarding the JFK assassination...we

48

are all told and taught to disregard what we see, hear or learn about any event (actual Science), and instead TRUST SOCIETY, RIGHT NOW, in every moment! Anything and everything else is a lie...a conspiracy by tin foil hat-wearing lunatics with nothing better to do! The same News-anchors and Newspaper writers that lapped up the nonsensical and ridiculous Warren Report as the LONE TRUTH regarding the lone assassin, represent the VERY SAME group of institutionalized music critics that tell us Bruce Hornsby is a jazz-inspired Pop artist that writes harmless songs with an annoying degree of "liberalism", end of story on Bruce Hornsby, buy his Greatest Hits package and go back to sleep America!

"Rock journalism is people who can't write, interviewing people who can't talk, in order to provide articles for people who can't read."
Frank Zappa

There are currently 150 albums in this series, each represented by an individual book. To my knowledge, such a thing has never been attempted, and I now understand why. This collection of books has taken me the better part of the last seven years of my life, writing around the clock because I felt such a sense of urgency to complete my task. I feel, and I hope you will too, that these books are NECESSARY as a push-back against everything that society has thrown at us over the last forty years. Since 1984, those that operate the music industry have taken back their control through a violent stranglehold. The prolific list of lush and creative music, the genius that was unleashed, almost uncontrollably, during the late Sixties/early Seventies, has now been viciously reigned back in by these tyrants of Century City. They started to take back control by creating the New Wave and Punk movements of the late

Seventies...and why was this effective? Because it was different...by 1977 a few corporations owned almost all of public radio...meaning, that they could "set the standards" for what could be played on air. And with the advent of that electronic garbage in the early eighties, the removal of the "last DJ", the death of GORGEOUS SOUNDING analogue tape, for the absolute sterile desolation of digital...they had all but squeezed out the greatest recording artists and bands in the history of popular music. Those artists that tried to continue through the Eighties were COERCED into releasing music that sounded dull, heartless and soulless...a hundred and eighty degrees from the albums they had created only a few years before. Again, why? Because had they not created these synthesizer-laden, digital wastelands, they wouldn't of had their records released. Only a HANDFUL of artists were able to maintain their integrity through the

Eighties, until such time that the smaller, independent record labels began to take shape in the late Eighties, early Nineties. I don't want to "name names" here, but I know you can instantly think of at least a dozen of your favorite bands that released disappointing/alarming albums...all with a vacuous, empty sound during this time period. But it is hard to blame the artists for this work when the entire industry shifted under their feet. Their personal trade, their life's passion was on the verge of being taken away from them...not to mention their source of income. Record companies weren't financing albums made in analogue-tape studios anymore, radio stations weren't programming "Classic Rock" on the Top Forty, so what choice did these artists really have? It was no different in Hollywood, the small collection of Directors that actually cared about telling the truth and the quality of what they were creating, were being reigned in as well. Hitchcock, Kubrick, Coppola, Lumet,

Oliver Stone, Warren Beatty, Ridley Scott, Woody Allen...even Clint Eastwood's low-budget, "home-movies" were being suppressed. And just ask Terry Gilliam how easy its been for him to find financial support every time he announces he is going to be making a film! So, in the face of all of this coercion, the lies and the restrictions on truth, it is my absolute pleasure and passion to resurrect the Rock and Roll album back to the integral, lofty heights it was meant to inhabit! The TRUTH about our reality found within the following list of records is staggering...its all here...not only a list of what is plaguing the world today, but also the simple solutions that will resolve our problems, forever, and set us free. This is why I believe this book series to be of such importance!

When it came time to settle upon a finite list, it was a task that was impossible for me to complete. At first, I thought 101 albums would be sufficient, but when it came time for final selections into this group, I simply couldn't do it, as I had close to 500 albums in my list! So, this was when I finally put some of my University knowledge and skills to good use (having three University Degrees, an undergraduate degree in Economics, an MBA, Masters of Business Administration, and a Teaching Degree so that I could teach this subject matter at the Collegiate level). In University I became a "wiz" in Microsoft Excel, the Spreadsheet program, where I built everything that I ever needed, especially for accounting, in Excel. Thus, to solve my dilemma over so many albums and my inability to decrease the size of the list to the absolute finest records, I created a complex spreadsheet to make my selections for me, adding in "scores" for each album, based upon the individual criterion I had developed. So, these albums had to be "perfect" in every way...(1) Musically, they had

to inspire, take chances and subvert
the norm in Rock and Roll
(something other than 2 chords, 1
change and a whole lotta "baby's"),
(2) Lyrically, they had to share
important truths about/for humanity,
and not promote Alistair Crowley and
Satanism, (3) these albums could
not possess even a single STINKER,
they all had to be great songs that
could be considered Classics, (4) the
songwriting had to feature
excellence, with creative writing
techniques that pushed the
boundaries of Rock music, (5) the
musical performances had to feature
excellence, there was zero tolerance
for bands or albums with musicians
who didn't possess the chops to play
complex musical creations, and (6)
the Production and Engineering of
the albums had to be CLEAN, FAT
and LUSCIOUS, while maintaining or
advancing the sound of the recording
process. Plus, double albums of
original material were weighted
higher than single albums. Thus,
when you look at those albums near

the top of my list, you really get a sense of what I was looking for. Jethro Tull's, Aqualung, was DIFFERENT (Ian Anderson is different). The songwriting was unique and spectacular, the music was complex and yet somehow accessible, and those lyrics, WOW! And how many Jethro Tull fans really even understand all of what he was powerfully saying? I mean, Locomotive Breath, SUBVERSION, and to me this is so important, and truly is the essence of what Rock and Roll was meant to be! So when I created these categories and entered in the raw data, Excel brought my list right down to near 150 albums! And once I had made those final difficult choices, I really began to examine this final list of 150 albums, and I noticed, right away, that subversion was what popped up everywhere, undermining the norm, often in the guise of artists and albums that didn't "seem" to be subversive...and of course the best examples of that are Steely Dan and

Joni Mitchell. Both wrote musical structures that turned conventional Rock music upside down, both pushed the boundaries of what was even considered possible with chords and sounds (Steely Dan with the "Mu Major" chord and Jazzy irregularities set to conventional arrangements...Joni Mitchell with bizarre tunings and odd finger patterns on her guitar that defied explanation..."Joni, what was that chord I just played, I'm not familiar with it"..."Uh, I don't know myself, I just invented it"). So if some Rock aficionados look down at this list with disdain because there is "Pop Music" or they don't understand it, already this series has served part of its purpose, which is to encourage people to think and look outside of the box, and to use critical thinking to decide things for themselves, instead of just taking what some "Rock Critic" said in an article for one of society's magazines, like, say, Rolling Stone magazine (which ISN'T subversive and represents the interests of the status quo). I realize on the surface that artists like, Styx, Billy Joel, Bruce Hornsby, Toto and Michael McDonald don't SEEM like Rock and Rollers, and perhaps shouldn't even be taken seriously, but we need to take another listen and to think again. These artists created "perfect" albums on this list in every way imaginable, and were very subversive in their musical and lyrical approaches. Does the average person even know what Toto's album, Hydra, was about? Do they care? And yet, you had skilled songwriters crafting perfect songs, with a degree of professionalism that few could ever match...speaking about who ruled over society, how they did it, and why the masses were ignorant to these facts (Really, I just thought it was about, about...hey honey, what time is American Gladiators on? I don't want to miss it")! Remember, Dylan himself taught an entire generation of songwriters that you can get away with murder by applying a little honey to a song, versus than always adding vinegar! Again, think of Steely Dan and albums like Aja and Gaucho, the height of "Yacht Rock" right? WRONG! These two albums were as subversive and unique as ANYTHING ever released, it's just that "someone" said in a magazine that this wasn't Rock and Roll, it was, well, boring...and yet, underneath the surface veneer of those painstakingly masterful creations, were some very, very dark truths about society! You just had to have the courage to look for them. How many of you have actually taken the time to listen to Bruce Hornsby songs like, Harbor Lights, Defenders of the Flag and Pastures of Plenty...you might be pleasantly surprised if you do! All written with chords, chord structures, rhythm sections, arrangements and performances that defied credulity. Did say the Stones ever do this or everyone's PRECIOUS Beatles? I wanted to create a list that best represented Excellence, Honesty,

Integrity and Subversion in Rock and Roll instead of the norm, the status quo, the same old thing...and NO ONE, EVER, will find such a list in anything that the Rolling Stone Magazine publishes. They TELL YOU what to believe in, what to think, how to act, what is "cool"...because they represent society, what is "hip" right now, and Scientism. Right or wrong, I represent the Individual, Integrity and God's Truth...which is the true essence of a band like, say, XTC, and the spirit of Rock and Roll!

One final note about my list of albums, you might be surprised by the repetition of so many artists on this list; there are a mere 70 different artists that are responsible for these 150 albums. However, after the list was completed, I came to understand why there were so many of these "repeat offenders"; this is because to achieve albums of this unrelenting quality, it takes not only natural genius, but countless areas of expertise. You simply cannot make albums the equal of these by simply being a talented "singer-songwriter". The quality of musicianship on these albums is PEERLESS by all but a select few. The Production, Engineering and Mastering of these albums is also what sets them apart. But ultimately, it came down to these albums being thematic masterpieces, where the music and lyrics were subtly woven strings that were simultaneously aware and sympathetic of the other's presence in every moment. Every note was perfectly placed in relation to the performance of the lyrics...each shared the same heartbeat as they meandered along, line by line. But the final qualification for selection was perhaps the "toughest" criterion of all...every song had to be an ascended creation...there was NO ROOM for filler on this list. A single "throw-away" song was enough to send a "worthy contender" falling from the list. And thus, only a few musicians in the history of music have ever possessed these combined abilities and the courage to create such absolute masterpieces! Perhaps the best example that I can give of this is The Who's masterpiece album, Who's Next (an album that saw Pete Townshend writing from way up within what Nikola Tesla described as the aether); it's perhaps the greatest collection of original songs on one album, all except for, My Wife, a John Entwistle composition that really had NO PLACE ON THIS ALBUM! Not that it's a "bad song", it's not...it's filled with a number of clever changes, benefits from superior playing by this gifted band of musicians, and some slick Production work, but it doesn't fit with the quality of Townshend's songwriting and the thematic message of Truth and Love by Pete Townshend. There was no way that this song was going to result in the album being stricken from the list; however, it did cause it to fall out of the "top ten", and maybe even the number one spot? Another track from the SAME PERIOD of songwriting for Townshend was, Long Live Rock. Now, if that song had replaced, My Wife, where does Who's Next stack up all time? It would be VERY tough to keep it from the top 5, for sure, and perhaps the very top itself! Now, a final thought about this list before I present it...I can assure you that I have no use for either agendas or labels. These albums, regardless of origin, BELONG here because they tell the truth, offer hope and do so with flawless songwriting, performances and production! I Love ALL MUSIC that has VALUE! Regardless of whether it is "soft" or "hard", fast-paced or slow. To me, an American band like X, with roots in the LA Punk Rock scene, sits perfectly at home on this list next to say Billy Joel or Elton John because their respective albums share A LOT in common with each other in terms of the care, quality and excellence, if not the sound!!! So without further ado, here is thy hallowed list, please enjoy, oh, and-a, LONG LIVE ROCK...

#1.Steely Dan, Aja, 1977
#2.Dan Fogelberg, The Innocent Age, 1981
#3.Frank Zappa & the Mothers of Invention, Freak Out! 1966
#4.Stevie Wonder, Songs in the Key of Life, 1976
#5.Pink Floyd, Dark Side of the Moon, 1973
#6.Bruce Springsteen, Born to Run, 1975
#7.George Harrison, All Things Must Pass, 1970
#8.Jethro Tull, Aqualung, 1971
#9.Todd Rundgren, Something/Anything? 1972
#10.Steely Dan, Countdown to Ecstasy, 1973
#11.Supertramp, Crime of the Century, 1974
#12.The Who, Who's Next, 1971
#13.Joni Mitchell, Court and Spark, 1974
#14.Sting, ...Nothing Like the Sun, 1987
#15.George Harrison, Living in the Material World, 1973
#16.Dire Straits, Love Over Gold, 1982
#17.Frank Zappa & the Mothers of Invention, We're Only in it For the Money, 1968
#18.The Clash, London Calling, 1979
#19.Earth, Wind & Fire, That's the Way of the World, 1975
#20.Sting, Dream of the Blue Turtles, 1985
#21.Stevie Wonder, Innervisions, 1973
#22.XTC, Nonsuch, 1992
#23.Steely Dan, Gaucho, 1980
#24.Bruce Springsteen, Darkness on the Edge of Town, 1978

#25.XTC, Skylarking, 1986
#26.Supertramp, Breakfast in America, 1979
#27.X, Under the Big Black Sun, 1982
#28.Creedence Clearwater Revival, Cosmos Factory, 1970
#29.Rush, Moving Pictures, 1981
#30.Traffic, The Low Spark of High Heeled Boys, 1971
#31.Steely Dan, Katy Lied, 1975
#32.John Mayer, Room For Squares, 2001
#33.Dire Straits, Making Movies, 1980
#34.Frank Zappa, Joe's Garage Acts I, II & III, 1979
#35.John Mayer, Continuum, 2006
#36.Al Stewart, Year of the Cat, 1976
#37.Donovan, Open Road, 1970
#38.Bruce Springsteen, The River, 1980
#39.Tears For Fears, Songs From the Big Chair, 1985
#40.Steely Dan, The Royal Scam, 1976
#41.XTC, Oranges and Lemons, 1989
#42.Dan Fogelberg, Phoenix, 1979
#43.Steely Dan, Pretzel Logic, 1974
#44.Supertramp, Even in the Quietest Moments, 1977
#45.Tom Petty & the Heartbreakers, The Last DJ, 2002
#46.Pink Floyd, Wish You Were Here, 1975
#47.Sting, The Soul Cages, 1991
#48.Steely Dan, Can't Buy a Thrill, 1972
#49.The Pretenders, Learning to Crawl, 1983
#50.Neil Young with Crazy Horse, Live Rust, 1979
#51.Robbie Robertson, Robbie Robertson, 1987
#52.The Who, Quadrophenia, 1973
#53.Joni Mitchell, The Hissing of Summer Lawns, 1975

#54.Joe Jackson, Night and Day, 1982
#55.Gino Vannelli, Brother to Brother, 1978
#56.Crosby, Stills, Nash & Young, Deja Vu, 1970
#57.The Alan Parsons Project, Turn of a Friendly Card, 1980
#58.The Police, Ghost in the Machine, 1981
#59.Stevie Wonder, Fulfillingness' First Finale, 1974
#60.Atlanta Rhythm Section, A Rock and Roll Alternative, 1976
#61.The Byrds, Fifth Dimension, 1966
#62.Tom Petty & the Heartbreakers, Hypnotic Eye, 2014
#63.John Lennon, Imagine, 1971
#64.Joni Mitchell, Hejira, 1977
#65.Lynyrd Skynyrd, Pronounced Leh-Nerd Skin-Nerd, 1973
#66.R.E.M. Automatic For the People, 1992
#67.Crosby, Stills & Nash, Crosby, Stills & Nash, 1969
#68.Bryan Ferry, In Your Mind, 1977
#69.Frank Zappa, Hot Rats, 1969
#70.Traffic, John Barleycorn Must Die, 1970
#71.Chicago, Chicago Transit Authority, 1969
#72.Creedence Clearwater Revival, Green River, 1969
#73.Elvis Costello, Imperial Bedroom, 1982
#74.Peter Gabriel, So, 1986
#75.Joe Jackson, Big World, 1986
#76.Roxy Music, Avalon, 1982
#77.Bruce Hornsby, Harbor Lights, 1993
#78.Talking Heads, Little Creatures, 1985
#79.Elvis Costello, This Year's Model, 1978
#80.Steppenwolf, Monster, 1979
#81.R.E.M. Monster, 1994
#82.Elvis Costello & Burt Bacharach, Painted From Memory, 1998

#83.The Guess Who, Share the Land, 1970
#84.Earth, Wind & Fire, All 'N All, 1977
#85.Donald Fagen, The Nightfly, 1982
#86.Van Morrison, Moondance, 1970
#87.Dire Straits, Dire Straits, 1978
#88.Flaunt the Imperfection, China Crisis, 1985
#89.Let's Dance, David Bowie, 1983
#90.Creedence Clearwater Revival, Willy and the Poor Boys, 1969
#91.The Byrds, Younger Than Yesterday, 1967
#92.The Doors, The Doors, 1967
#93.Yes, The Yes Album, 1971
#94.Neil Young with Crazy Horse, Everybody Knows This is Nowhere, 1969
#95.Steve Forbert, Alive on Arrival, 1978
#96.China Crisis, Warped by Success, 1994
#97.The Doobie Brothers, The Captain and Me,
#98.David Bowie, The Rise and Fall of Ziggy Stardust, 1972
#99.Stevie Wonder, Talking Book, 1972
#100.The Band, The Brown Album, 1969
#101.Styx, The Grand Illusion, 1977
#102.The Beatles, Abbey Road, 1969
#103.The Alan Parsons Project, I Robot, 1977
#104.Billy Joel, The Nylon Curtain, 1982
#105.X, More Fun in the New World, 1983
#106.Pink Floyd, The Wall, 1979
#107.Rush, Permanent Waves, 1980
#108.Bruce Hornsby & the Range, The Way it is, 1986
#109.Carole King, Tapestry, 1971
#110.Creedence Clearwater Revival, Bayou Country, 1969
#111.Elton John, Goodbye Yellow Brick Road, 1973
#112.Toto, Toto IV, 1982
#113.Al Stewart, Time Passages, 1978

#114.The Alan Parsons Project, Pyramid, 1978
#115.Yes, Fragile, 1972
#116.John Lennon, Plastic Ono Band, 1970
#117.The Police, Synchronicity, 1983
#118.Elvis Costello, Punch the Clock, 1983
#119.Bryan Ferry, Boys and Girls, 1985
#120.Michael Franks, Tiger in the Rain, 1979
#121.Rickie Lee Jones, Pirates, 1981
#122.Warren Zevon, Excitable Boy, 1978
#123.Lynyrd Skynyrd, Second Helping, 1974
#124.Dire Straits, Brothers in Arms, 1985
#125.Frank Zappa & the Mothers of Invention, Absolutely Free, 1967
#126.The Beatles, Revolver, 1966
#127.Steely Dan, Two Against Nature, 2000
#128.Al Stewart, 24 Carrots, 1980
#129.The Beatles, Sgt. Pepper's Lonely Hearts Club Band, 1967
#130.The Allman Brothers Band, The Allman Brothers Band, 1969
#131.Frank Zappa, Sheik Yerbouti, 1979
#132.Styx, Pieces of Eight, 1978
#133.Earth, Wind & Fire, Head to the Sky, 1973
#134.Tom Petty & the Heartbreakers, Mojo, 2010
#135.Van Morrison, His Band & the Street Choir, 1970
#136.Toto, Hydra, 1979
#137.The Pretenders, Last of the Independents, 1994
#138.Atlanta Rhythm Section, Champagne Jam, 1978
#139.Michael Jackson, Thriller, 1982
#140.Todd Rundgren, Runt: The Ballad of Todd Rundgren, 1971
#141.Billy Joel, River of Dreams, 1993
#142.Steve Winwood, Back in the High Life, 1986

#143.Donald Fagen, Morph the Cat, 2006
#144.Michael McDonald, If That's What it Takes, 1982
#145.The Doors, Strange Days, 1968
#146.Atlanta Rhythm Section, Third Annual Pipe Dream, 1974
#147.Joe Jackson, Look Sharp! 1978
#148.Steppenwolf, Steppenwolf, 1967
#149.Steve Winwood, Arc of a Diver, 1980
#150.Pablo Cruise, World's Away, 1978

"To learn who rules over you, simply find out who you are not allowed to criticize."
Voltaire

"It is no measure of health to be well-adjusted to a profoundly sick society."
Jiddu Krishnamurti

"All truth passes through three stages. First, it is ridiculed. Second, it is violently opposed. Third, it is accepted as being self-evident."
Arthur Schopenhauer

"The decisive question for man is: Is he related to something infinite or not? That is the telling question of his life. Only if we know that the thing which truly matters is the infinite can we avoid fixing our interests upon futilities, and upon all kinds of goals which are

not of real importance. Thus we demand that the world grant us recognition for qualities which we regard as personal possessions: our talent or our beauty. The more a man lays stress on false possessions, and the less sensitivity he has for what is essential, the less satisfying is his life. He feels limited because he has limited aims, and the result is envy and jealousy. If we understand and feel that here in this life we already have a link with the infinite...desires and attitudes change."
Carl Jung

DEDICATIONS

This book series is dedicated to my entire family and the vibration of Love, who are my world...here's KNOWING that they will always be with me, through Love:

Colleen, Spencer, Sionade, Jordan, Bob, Armando, Buttercup, Samwise Gamgee, Radagast, Frodo, Lola, Arwen, Indiana, Taquito, Gimli, Tauriel, Legolas, Luthien, Canela, Phryne, Dottie, Sherlock, Watson, Rosie Cotton, Radar, Bilbo, Murphy, Goldberry, Luna, Guinnevere & Strider!

I wish to especially mention those that have transitioned to our non-physical realm during the writing of this book series:

Audrey, Aurora, Aragorn, Galadriel, Linky, Jenny, Merlin, Jackson and most recently, Pippin...you are all my precious angels and I will see you once again, just not yet!

To my precious wife, partner, friend and confidant...Colleen. It is only through your beautiful selflessness that this massive project has become a reality. All that I am is yours...FOREVERMORE!

ALBUM INFORMATION

Album #69 in the Series

Frank Zappa

Hot Rats

1969, Producer Frank Zappa

"Jazz isn't dead, it just smells funny."

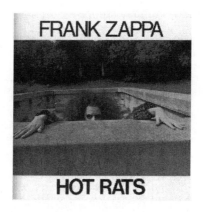

Previous Album:
Uncle Meat (1969)

Follow Up Album:
Burnt Weeny Sandwich (1970)

Other Must Hear Albums:
Freak Out, Absolutely Free, We're
Only In It For the Money, Uncle
Meat, 200 Motels, The Grand
Wazoo, Over-Nite Sensation,
Apostrophe, Roxy and Elsewhere,
One Size Fits All, Zoot Allures, Sheik
Yerbouti, Joe's Garage, Shut Up 'n
Play Yer Guitar series, Jazz From
Hell, The Lost Episodes, The Yellow
Shark

Chart Positions:
US #173
Holland#6
UK#9

Singles: None

ALBUM COVER/ART DESIGN

"When I first met Zappa in New York, the art studio was in his apartment, but that was only for a brief period. I didn't actually live there (as widely reported), but I would commute to work at his place. When we moved to LA he had rented the log cabin, I had a wing of it. It was my living quarters and art studio, which I rented from them."

Cal Schenkel

Frank Zappa was a true artist, and as such, he was very involved with his friend, artist Cal Schenkel, on generating the ideas and designs for all aspects of his album packages. No musical artist ever understood the value of an entire album package better than Frank Zappa. Frank never wasted the opportunity of space to describe his music (thus himself) to the listener; therefore, every aspect of his albums bore messages…from the front and back covers, to the gatefolds and record sleeves.

Graphic images, lyrics, production information, quotes, or just general thoughts/ramblings invariably found their way onto every portion of his albums, making every Zappa record an almost surreal experience, each with different themes or "feels".

The Hot Rats album package was one Zappa's finest and the album cover remains easily one of the most iconic ever in Rock music history! On the cover, the Zappa family's "Nanny" and Groupie, Christine Frka (aka Miss Christine of the GTO's), was photographed by LA photographer Andee Cohen Nathanson coming out of a "crypt" on the property of "The Log House", which Zappa was renting at the time in Laurel Canyon. The image gave the impression of some subversive, subterranean creature crawling out from the underbelly of society. The crypt was actually an opening for the property's sewer/septic system, and as such one could also easily view the cover as a rat coming out of a sewer as well. Thus, the thematic tone for the album was already well established even before a single song had been played. Hot Rats reflected a psychedelic society where citizens were trying to find their way, all struggling for fame and the "American Dream", from the bowels of a giant cesspool. Nathanson used color IR (infrared) film to create the "out-of-this-world", psychedelic look. By taking the photo near ground level he was able to make the crypt look a lot bigger than it actually was and created an effective backdrop with the bizarre red foliage! Cal Schenkel encompassed this psychedelic look throughout the package and it tied in well with the groundbreaking musical approach of the album, Schenkel commented years later…

"I liked working in a lot of different directions and doing very eclectic stuff and working in different styles, and Frank was doing that with his music."

As with all of their album art collaborations, Zappa and Schenkel combined their artistic creativity to produce a unique and memorable album package. They had set the "creativity bar" very high on We're Only in it for the Money, Cruising with Ruben and the Jets and Uncle Meat, but Hot Rats held its own. The album art conveyed Zappa's message of a pseudo-pyschedelic experience and made it clear that this was a Zappa record with the help of Ian Underwood, and not a Mothers of Invention album. Another classic of Frank Zappa's album art!

ALBUM OVERVIEW

So that most readers will continue on from here and read the entire book, I'm not going to tell you the name of the artist that created this "most groovy" album. Why you ask? Because most music fans think his sound is ugly and too weird, and wish to have nothing to do with it and the crazed minority this music represents. However, the album is really, really spiffy…it has lots of pictures all over it and if you hold the album in a certain way, in a certain light, it turns black and white right there in front of your eyes. Thus, it is imperative that you acquire this album and discover this exciting composer, this daring arranger, this, this, reasonably competent guitar player, who must unfortunately remain anonymous during the review of this album…or not?

Photograph by **Andee Cohen Nathanson** of
"the Hot Rat", Christine Frka

For most music fans and critics
muddled within the dizzying times of
1969, Hot Rats came as quite a
shock, from deep out of "right field",
but it shouldn't have been viewed as
such a surprise. Zappa and the
Mothers of Invention had recorded
five albums together in just under

81

three years; four of which were incredibly complex albums to record (and produce)! During this time Zappa also released his first solo record, Lumpy Gravy, the Nick Venet/Capitol Records project of orchestral music written and conducted by Zappa (he wasn't allowed to play on the record as per his recording contract with Verve/MGM). This album alone featured an HOUR of recorded orchestral music! The fact was that Zappa was being pushed to his limit during these first three years of his music career (on top of which he and Gail were beginning their own family). During this time very few "Rock" bands were talked about or respected as much as Zappa and the Mothers (even though none of their albums pushed past the Top Thirty)! When they toured together the money for everyone in the ever-growing band was good, as Frank Zappa and the Mothers of Invention were perhaps the most requested live act across the Earth by 1968.

Zappa and the Mothers played sold out concerts across Europe, often open-air venues, that were filled with their rabid fans that were dying to see them play live. However, Zappa simply could NOT tour a lot and this put an enormous amount of pressure on the Mother's personnel because they were not writing the songs, this was the sole providence of Zappa; thus, they were either in recording studios or at home for long periods of time using up all the money they made while on the road. This wasn't as big a problem for Frank because he was receiving all the record royalties; plus, with his burgeoning family and the fact that his first Loves were composing and creating music (like Becker and Fagen from Steely Dan), the studio was his home...which became the literal truth when the Utility Muffin Research Kitchen was fully completed at his home in Laurel Canyon in 1979!

During the recording sessions for the very complex album, Uncle Meat (the on again/off again sessions took a year to complete), tempers began to boil over in the studio between Zappa and the Mother's band who were beginning to resent his press, supposed riches, idiosyncratic nature and Rock and Roll "stature". Also, Zappa did not use many of the Mothers on the studio tracks for the album, We're Only in it For the Money. Zappa captured all of this angst on the "song" If We'd All Been Living in California…which was a taped conversation between he and drummer Jimmy Carl Black ("hi boys and girls, I'm Jimmy Carl Black and I'm the Indian of the group") regarding how seldom the Mothers toured, and how little money they were making over the confines of an entire year. All of this began to take a toll on Zappa's patience and shortly after the completion of Uncle Meat he severed his ties with The Mothers. Which, at the time, shocked the members of the band because, as mentioned earlier, they were one of, if not THE most respected and sought-after live acts on Earth...but Zappa was done, for the time-being, with the Mothers moniker.

After the New Year, Frank settled into the writing and recording his second solo album, the heavily Jazz influenced, Hot Rats. Throughout his first six albums, Frank had demonstrated his interest in Jazz with not only the music, but with the song structures as well. So for some, the Jazz influences on Hot Rats weren't such a huge surprise, but the seamless combination of Jazz and Rock was...as the sounds were truly pioneering! Hot Rats went far beyond the Jazz inspired recordings of The Byrds, Pink Floyd and Cream. The first actual sources of Jazz/Fusion came from The Garry Burton Quartet's 1967 album, Duster (featuring guitarist Larry Coryell); also from Miles Davis' 1968 album,

Miles in the Sky. Then in early 1969 the band Chicago released their first album, Chicago Transit Authority, which directly fused elements of Jazz, Blues, Brass and R&B to Rock music and Rock music song structures. But it was Zappa that took all of these noble beginnings and really defined the genre with Hot Rats. The album featured only six tracks, largely consisting of instrumental Jazz-influenced compositions with extensive soloing (Zappa on guitar, Ian Underwood on Saxes, Reeds and Keyboards and Don "Sugarcane" Harris and Jean-Luc Ponty on electric violin). The only song that contained vocals was Willie the Pimp, which consisted of a brief lyrical section (sung by childhood friend, Captain Beefheart) and then was dominated by a lengthy and brilliant extended guitar solo by Zappa. His first five albums with the Mothers were dominated by brief, parody-type songs (with lots of Jazzy chords thrown into the melodies) that were highly satirical in nature with multiple vocals and the incorporation of "musique concrete" through a long editing process. Hot Rats turned away from his satire and controversial truth-telling lyrics and put the focus on his compositions, along with the quality of the musical performances. To this end, the only "Mother" that Zappa brought along with him was Ian Underwood ("the straight member of the group") who possessed the variability and chops to play these complex and demanding songs. After Zappa and Underwood, Frank hired session musicians and Jazz-based performers to fill out his tight roster. Don "Sugarcane" Harris (Frank was a huge fan of his growing up) and French born Jean-Luc Ponty played violin on the album (which included extensive soloing), the brilliant Max Bennett handled the bass throughout (Shuggie Otis played the the rollicking bass track on Peaches en Regalia, which was a dream come true for Zappa) and the combination of John Guerin, Paul Humphrey and

Ron Selico sat in the legendary Zappa drum seat.

Not only was the music breaking new territory (and barriers), but Zappa recorded the album on a brand new, state-of-the-art, 16-track analogue recording console, which allowed him to layer these numbers with supporting tracks that added to each song's ambience. Zappa described the 16-track recorder as "homemade"; in truth, the engineers at TTG Studios in Hollywood worked around the clock to customize their newest creation to the specs that Zappa needed for the recording of the album. As such, much of the album was recorded at TTG Studios. It was this machine, seen below, that allowed Frank to become the "overdub enthusiast" that he became, especially for his guitar solos, as he preferred the tonal sounds he created live to what he was able to achieve within the sterility of the studio...

The MM-1000 16-Track Analogue Tape
Recorder by TTG Studios

And did Zappa ever put the MM-
1000 to good use on the album;
besides all of the overdubbing that
he used to complete each song's
purposeful layering, he used the new
technology for a great deal of other

techniques. Hot Rats saw Zappa become the first recording artist, ever, to record each song's drum performance on multiple tracks...the result was a "stereo drum sound". Before Hot Rats, the industry recorded each song's drum performance directly to a single mono-track of an 8-track recording machine. However, on Hot Rats, Zappa had the engineers at TTG assign four of the machine's tracks to capture the whole of the drum performance...individual tracks for the snare and bass drums and left/right tracks for the remaining drums, toms and cymbals. This allowed Zappa and his own engineer, Dick Kunc, to work closely with the TTG Engineers to create incredibly accurate and realistic drum sounds that set Hot Rats apart from ANY OTHER Rock and Roll album to that point in recorded music history. It wasn't long after Hot Rats, that this recording technique with the drum kit became the standard all around the world...and is still featured today!

Zappa then manipulated with the various speed settings on the 16-track recorder to create unique, often bizarre timbres and tones. These can be best heard on the songs, Peaches en Regalia, Son of Mr. Green Genes and It Must be a Camel...where Zappa recorded the entire rhythm sections of these songs at "fast" speed; while adding the remaining percussive overdubs in while these basic tracks were being played back at "half" speed. Thus, on these songs, all of the percussive overdubs STAND OUT and help to drive the unusual, often other-worldly sounds that really make Hot Rats a ONE-OFF production. Zappa then repeated this recording method with many of the keyboard, saxophone and bass tracks (as heard with his "Octave Bass" on Peaches). Zappa even integrated a processed electronic organ sound to become part of an orchestral ensemble that featured Underwood's piano and various woodwinds. He also recorded himself playing both a plastic comb and a ratchet-wrench that were manipulated by the MM-1000...ALL these things were done by Zappa at the BEGINNING of ANALOGUE recording technology, MORE THAN A DECADE before the advent of digital sound processing devices!!! Think about this for a second...not only was the album ground-breaking in terms of producing the first Rock and Roll Fusion record, but Zappa created a tonal and timbre quality to the album that HAS NEVER BEEN MATCHED since...not even by Zappa himself. Thus, every time you listen to the Hot Rats album, there is an eternal sense of freshness and rareness about it. How many other albums can you actually say this about? For each song, Zappa took a tight-knit group of seasoned Jazz musicians and practiced with them around the clock until they, as a rhythm-section quartet, began to jam with the musical-stylings of a Blues Band, and set about to perform these odd tracks with a straight-ahead, 4x4 Rock and Roll sentimentality! It just doesn't get any better or weirder than this!

Peaches en Regalia became the perfect example of what Zappa could create sonically, as a brilliant record Producer, using cutting-edge technology. He used all sixteen tracks (and his other "editing" techniques) to construct a "simple Pop song" that featured complex layers of Underwood's reed and horn parts and his own various guitar fills. On an album that is known for its unique sounds, Peaches stands alone in terms of its originality! This began a long, creative and prolific run for Zappa in the studio showing off his prowess, especially with all of his overdubs (which is what essentially allowed him to release so many of his original songs from live concerts onto his "studio-made" albums). His Arranging of the album also matched his Production and Engineering work. Whenever Zappa wanted to, he was able to lead his seasoned Jazz players into very "down and dirty" Rock and Blues grooves (e.g. Willie the Pimp and Son of Mr. Green Genes) that fit with both John Lee Hooker and the Allman Brothers; while also seamlessly fitting very complex Jazz chords and rhythms into what were essentially three-minute Pop song structures (e.g. Peaches, Little Umbrellas). After a couple of listens, the song, Peaches en Regalia, sounded like something you might hear on the radio next to songs from Sgt. Peppers or Pet Sounds. Certainly his more experimental jams (The Gumbo Variations and It Must Be a Camel) were very jazz-orientated, but on "Gumbo" the Sugarcane Harris violin solo was played with heavy Rock and Roll overtones that rolled into the sizzling Zappa guitar solo, which segued effortlessly into a brief, but funky drum fill by Paul Humphrey and then the Max Bennett Bass solo…very funky, bluesy and gritty for a sixteen-minute Jazz improvisation! The result of all this was one of the finest Rock and Roll albums in music history, regardless of the genre! An album that not only helped to solidify the legitimate musical genre of Jazz/Rock Fusion, but really laid out many of the parameters for the Prog-Rock movement that was soon to follow. This is why the Hot Rats album sits at #69 on this list…every time you try to label it Jazz, it's a Blues record, if not Blues, then a dirty and gritty Rock and Roll jam…all the while laying out the basic elements for Progressive Rock BEFORE there was Prog-Rock! Frank Zappa is, and will always be…THE MAN!

Clearly the album inspired a great deal of artists looking to sow and reap rich, new territory…just how many we will never know, but an album like The Low Spark of High Heeled Boys for instance was a direct result of this union of musical styles. British bands, in particular the Beatles and Cream, were floored by the what they heard was possible musically within the format of a three-minute Pop song and forced them to take a deeper look at what they were creating musically. There are obvious influences in bands like Jethro Tull, Pink Floyd, Traffic, Steely Dan, Yes and Elvis Costello, but also less obvious influences in artists such as Joni Mitchell, The Byrds, Roxy Music and Bryan Ferry, the Talking Heads, Gino Vannelli, Joe Jackson, The Pretenders, Ricki Lee Jones, and even the likes of Sting, Bruce Hornsby, the Guess Who, Chicago and David Bowie. But perhaps the greatest legacy of all from this album was Zappa's guitar work. To this point in his career, Zappa had sacrificed his guitar prowess to create all those stylistic, satirical two-minute Pop gems. We knew from his body of work on the

Freak Out album that Zappa was a good guitar player, but he rarely demonstrated it, as with Trouble Every Day. After Hot Rats, his guitar became more and more the staple behind his run of brilliant, groundbreaking albums. On an album like Chunga's Revenge, for example, Zappa showcased his peerless skills in creating sonic masterpieces in very much a Rock and Roll setting (Transylvania Boogie, Road Ladies, Tell Me You Love Me, Chunga's Revenge), which foreshadowed all those legendary solos to come (such as Zombie Woof, Inca Roads, On the Bus and Watermelon in Easter Hay). The song Willie the Pimp featured an intense Howlin' Wolf-like vocal by Captain Beefheart for about a minute and a half before Zappa soloed through the rest of the song (EIGHT minutes), rarely repeating his guitar runs as he remained technically perfect, creatively fresh and sonically enlightened! Son of Mr. Green Genes and The Gumbo Variations featured more creative, interpretive solos, while "Peaches" and It Must Be a Camel witnessed very difficult, technical runs and fills, with incredibly melodic parts. Zappa announced with a bang to the rest of the music world that he was as good as a guitar player as he was a composer, producer, engineer and arranger…and there have only been a precious few that have ever matched Frank at these levels!

Zappa at the Log Cabin, in Laurel Canyon, circa 1969

TRACK 1 - PEACHES EN REGALIA

"The name of this song is called 'Peaches En Regalia.' It tells the story of a bowl of peaches that lives in the Royal Garden Hotel, across the street from the Kensington Market in London." FZ, 1969

The record opened with the quintessential track from the album, Peaches en Regalia. Frank dedicated the song (and the album) to his month old son, Dweezil, and described the record as a "movie for your years", which adeptly summed it up as the music encouraged you to close your eyes and use your imagination. The song epitomized what was so "right" about this album as its Jazz and Rock elements flowed along together, seamlessly, with ease. It was clearly a song constructed from a Jazz perspective, filled with Jazzy chords and musical progression, but everything else about the song was done from a Rock and Roll mindset. This track was one of the four songs (Peaches, Son of Mr. Green Genes, Little Umbrellas and It Must Be a Camel) that were fully written out for the musicians that featured scripted melodies that were designed to fit within specific time limits. Zappa purposefully structured these songs to give them Rock and Roll elements (such as 4x4 time) and had each rhythm section played by a "Rock" quartet. There are many people that view Peaches en Regalia (Peaches and Cream) as a Pop song without lyrics, which is a profound compliment to its author.

Dweezil, Gail and FZ...Peaches en Regalia,
how precious is one's family?

The song has become widely
regarded as perhaps THE Jazz/Rock
Fusion standard and it's part of "The
Real Book" (the "underground",
unlicensed compilation of the finest
Jazz songs in history, which includes
not only the chords and lyrics, but
the actual lead sheets...musicians

101

and band leaders love working from this book because it comes in different editions in a variety of keys, all with the exact same page sequences and numbers!). For Zappa's hybrid song to be in this book demonstrates not only the tremendous respect Frank's music receives from all musical genres, but just how impressive the writing of this song is!

The song opened with the iconic drum fill performed by Ron Selico. It has become one of the most famous drum intros in music history and only outdone in Zappa's catalogue by the intro to Montana. Whether re-done by Frank himself or a bevy of cover-artists, that drum fill has remained in each version of the song throughout time. Out of interest, Zappa's first instrument was the snare drum, and his first composition, (written at age 13), was a solo drum piece entitled Mice. Frank had a life-long passion for percussion and actually wrote-out the drum charts on most of his songs creating, without a doubt, the greatest body of drum work in music history…and that my friends is a profound compliment to bestow upon Zappa, as the body of excellent percussive work that exists is quite large and includes the works of Steely Dan. Zappa's Production and Engineering work with the multi-tracking of the Peaches drum sound is also legendary. Peaches set the bench-mark for studio recording of drum tracks that still exists today. Also, Zappa was one of the very first artists to tour with multiple percussionists and was the first to record in-studio with two drummers. The men who have sat on Zappa's drum chair literally represent the who's who of Rock and Roll drummers (Terry Bozzio, Vinnie Colaiuta, Ansley Dunbar, John Guerin, Jim Gordon, Paul Humphrey, Ralph Humphrey, Chad Wackerman and Chester Thompson to name just a few).

Terry Bozzio performing Punky's Whips live

After the drum intro, the band jumped in and essentially performed a Pop song, with an Intro, Verse, Chorus, Verse, Break, extended Solo, Break, Verse and Outro…all in 4x4 time! In fact, most of Hot Rats was performed in 4x4 with only the song, It Must Be a Camel, varying between a disguised 4x4 and 6x4 time. This was done on purpose by Frank as these 4x4 grooves kept the arrangements tight and the performances sounding cohesive…a real "band" sound. The brilliant LA musician Shuggie Otis played a wonderfully melodic bass line, but the song was dominated by Zappa and the Mothers of Invention sideman, Ian Underwood. What often gets lost in the song is Zappa's incredible acoustic guitar work (alongside Underwood's beautiful Flute), which gave the track a very Earthy sensibility next to its otherworldliness! Frank also soloed during the first verse with an "Octave" Bass, which was a conventional bass guitar recorded at half-speed so it sounded an octave higher than normal during playback. But it was really Ian Underwood who shined as a performer on this song. After the Hot Rats album was released internationally, he became known world-wide as a master-musician, especially from this song, dominating its sound with his dual Alto and Tenor Saxophone solos, his Piano, Electric Piano, Synthesizer, Clarinet, and Flute work! None of it came off as overly technical or heartless; Underwood played with a great deal of passion and playfulness, which defined the song's sound. It would be shortsighted to describe Underwood's performances here as his best ever, but they were certainly at or near the top of his incredible list!

Frank in the Studio for the recording of the Hot Rats album, 1969

Again, the creation of the 16-track

recorder for this album was a key. On Peaches alone, Zappa was able to layer more than a half-dozen of Underwood's subtle backing tracks to help accentuate the lead instruments, especially the sax. If recorded a year earlier this song simply would not have sounded anywhere near the same; thus, it was another example of art pushing the boundaries of technology, and technology forcing itself to find a way to catch up. Zappa was also able to create the first "stereo sounding" drums on vinyl in history, by devoting four tracks to the drum performance (with individual recording of the snare and bass drums, and left/right tracks featuring the toms and cymbals), giving Zappa engineer, Dick Kunc, an unprecedented ability to set each take a little differently on the final mix giving the drums a true stereo, other-worldly sound. Kunc and Zappa's engineering work on Peaches set the standard for drum recording techniques that still stands today!

There is also a great deal of synchronicity that surrounds Peaches en Regalia as a song...from Frank dedicating it to his new-born son, Dweezil, to Dweezil and his band, Zappa Plays Zappa, winning the 2009 Grammy-award for their version of the song! In his acceptance speech Dweezil said, fighting back tears...

"Did you feel it? The world actually fell off its axis...this particular song means a lot to me, it's 40 years old and it's on a record that was dedicated to me when I was born, so I'm dedicating it right back."

And through this energy of Love, Excellence and Dedication, that surrounds the song, it has remained un-ravaged by the passages of the Rock and Roll industry...it's a song that is the poster child for everything that is "right" in this world and what Rock and Roll music was meant to be...and it's one of my all-time favorite songs! As I fight back tears, thank you Frank and thank you Dweezil!

In actuality it was Steve Vai who taught Dweezil to play the guitar, and in case you didn't know this...Dweezil Zappa is a stunningly good guitarist! Why am I not surprised???

TRACK 2 – WILLIE THE PIMP

"I was overdubbing the solo while standing in the control room. The guitar was going into the board, out of the board, into the studio, into the amp, picked up by a microphone and back into the board. I'm playing my wah-wah pedal and wailing away, and this guy from the union comes in. He's standing behind me, tapping his pencil on his clipboard, waiting for me to get done so that he can ask me whether or not I've filed some kind of union paper about how many musicians I'm using. That's the solo on the record, and the whole time there was this union pood-head standing behind me." FZ, 1985

Frank Zappa and Don Van Vliet (Captain Beefheart) circa Hot Rats

Willie the Pimp came next, and while it was a vast departure from the flowing, otherworldliness of Peaches, it was also the album's centerpiece message. The record's title came from Captain Beefheart's ad-lib on the girls in Willie the Pimp being "hot meat", which was probably an easy choice of words for Zappa as during his time in New York he came to know all about rats (both the human and rodent kinds)! There were some commonalities between "Willie" and "Peaches", as they were both played in 4/4 time and gave the feeling of tight song structures that allowed for extended soloing. However, after this, the comparisons ended...if Peaches en Regalia was celebrating all that human beings were capable of creating, then Willie the Pimp was its 180 degree opposite! "Willie" was a representation of humanity at its worst.

From the moment that Don "Sugarcane" Harris played the song's principle melody, alone, on the Violin (in what can only be described as RAW), you got the sense that the music was going to be as greasy and gritty as the song's namesake...

Don "Sugarcane" Harris live

And when the whole band jumped in, along with Captain Beefheart's vocal, the creepiness of the song's main character was fully revealed through the driving, bluesy, Rock and Roll groove. However, while the song's origins were firmly rooted in the Blues and the melody was a written-out 4x4 Rock and Roll piece, Zappa structured the song very much like a Jazz improvisation to allow for his epic electric guitar solo. It was comprised as an intro, followed by the verse, with a brief refrain before Beefheart had two goes at the song's chorus (with a kind of vocal solo in between with all of his hooting and hollering). From there, Zappa soloed over the rest of the track with bassist, Max Bennett and drummer, John Guerin providing superb performances that were seemingly as concerned with improvisations as they were at keeping the rhythm of the song; and yet, somehow, it all fell into place and worked. So, really, the song was pure Rock and Roll...no, wait, it was a Power-Trio Blues...no, it was clearly a lengthy Jazz-inspired Jam...wait, what?

Looking back at Zappa's legendary guitar solo now, it appears as yet another Zappa sonic masterpiece; however, at the time, Zappa hadn't included a lot of guitar solos on those original Mother's records (Hungry Freaks and Trouble Every Day???), and had not explored the powerful harmonics that electric guitars could make, especially either run through the mixing board, or through a foot pedal (the first actual foot pedal, designed for the Vox Continental organ was created in 1966). This song represented the first time that Zappa brought his deep understanding of harmonics to the electric guitar with a mesmerizing sound that took you deep within yourself and your own imagination. It's actually difficult to

114

decide which was better, his incredible guitar riffs and chops or the song's sonic tonal quality? For seven storied minutes, Frank explored the song's melody with run after run on his modified Gibson Goldtop, without ever repeating a single expression, all the while expanding upon the guitar's tonal quality! Rolling Stone magazine has this solo ranked at #75 all-time of the greatest guitar solos (although at one time it was ranked as high as #17). So, for all fans of the Mothers, this song, this performance, and the album in general, was a massive awakening into the world of what Frank Zappa was capable of on the electric guitar...a portal of things to come...and if Zappa was already "well thought of" world-wide before Hot Rats, his legend grew to epic proportions after this album's release...this is when his persona began to take on those "larger-than-life" dimensions!

For the Hot Rats album, the iconoclastic Zappa severely altered his 1952 P-90 Goldtop original, modifying the P-90 neck with a single coil Humbucker pickup, a Bigsby tremelo tailpiece and an expanded tonal palette via six rotary controls. There were people at the time that thought Zappa was crazy to "mess up" this very rare Gibson Goldtop, but of course in life if you don't take "risks" or challenges then you never know what you are capable of, and what is possible…and the legendary sonic results from the album wouldn't have existed…and as a side-note, this exact guitar, with all of its modifications, was sold at an auction for a six-figure sum in 2007.

Captain Beefheart, off of the Hot Rats inner
gatefold, with L. Ron Hoover's Vacuum
Cleaner...apparently...

Essentially Willie the Pimp was a
fairly-tight, two-and-a-half minute
Blues/Rock song that had a seven-
minute guitar solo added on to it. By
the time that Captain Beefheart had
finished his idiosyncratic vocal,
complete with his "whoops and
yelps" solo, Zappa "whipped out" a
message to his friend and guitar-

mentor, Eric Clapton (and his band, Cream), that Zappa had arrived on the scene as a top guitar soloist and the leader of his own powerful Rock trio. Zappa's Power Trio of himself on guitar, Max Bennett on bass and John Guerin on drums, created a Rock and Roll jam that was as good as ANYTHING ever generated within any genre of popular music! The song wasn't just Frank's solo…like any great Jazz improvisation, or musical trio, the players fed off of one another. All three of them were soloing within their collective parts! Just listen to Guerin's drumbeat, as the song blistered along…he not only kept perfect time, but turned his performance into one laden with fills and creative expressions. How many Rock and Roll drum performances were better than this one? The same was true for Max Bennett who provided a very funky rhythm that got more and more aggressive as the song progressed because he was feeding off of Zappa's solo and Guerin's energy. These three defined "being in the moment", which IS JAZZ, and improvised an extended jam that sounds as good today as it did in 1969! Willie the Pimp also dispelled the lies spread over the years that hiring session musicians resulted in slick, but heartless music...completely untrue...as Guerin and Bennett blew that bullshit out of the water! Listening to Zappa's solo is a purely sublime experience and it always amazes me just how fast seven minutes can go by! It was a performance, like a good red wine, that simply got better and better with age. In 1969, Rock and Roll guitar was dominated by the likes of Jimi Hendrix, Duane Allman, Jeff Beck, Eric Clapton, Roger McGuinn, Dick Dale, Jimmy Page, Stephen Stills and Neil Young, but with his performances on Hot Rats, Zappa catapulted himself to this level, and alongside perhaps only Hendrix and Allman, as the best Rock and Roll guitarists in history at creating in-the-moment sonic masterpieces that transcended the listener into different vibrations and even to different personal dimensions!

Zappa's lyrical story for the song was partly based upon his own experiences coming and going from his first hotel in New York City, while he and The Mothers were holding court at the Garrick Theatre on Bleecker Street; the details of the story came from a conversation he had with some of his Garrick friends, Annie and Cynthia...

Annie Zannas: "Son-of-a-bitch, you did this one, you did that one," he told me
FZ: How could you do this to him?
Annie: I told him that I did something and I was happy for doing it, you know, I'm happy now, I don't care, you know, what you think. "You are happy? I'm more happy than anyone" he said; meanwhile, he's sittin' there completely miserable, tellin' me that he's more happy than the whole house put together, he has more intelligence than the whole house put together, and he's sitting there with his dumb words, "Oh, you son-of-a-bitch, you're a schmuck and you're a

schmuck," nothing, you know, nice about people, 'cause all people is shitty to him, you know, and I tried to explain to, I says, but they're not, you know? It's just how you take 'em, I mean, he's . . .

FZ: Why do you call him 'Willie The Pimp'?

Annie: Oh, because we, just imagined uh, him . . . wait--

Cynthia Dobson: The Lido Hotel.

Annie: Oh, yeah, the Lido Hotel, this perverted hotel in Coney Island, really perverted. So we made up this story about my mother um , ha-ha, calling up Willie telling that we're a woman uh, body shapes ah, 38-25-40 or something like that, some bizarre shape, blonde hair and all decked out insanely and um, tell him to meet us in front of the uh, Lido Hotel. And, ha-ha, then we, what we were gonna do, if we really would do this, like we'll make sure, we'll see him like, you know, casually leave the house at this certain time and we'll know that, you know, he's leaving to meet this woman, that's not gonna be there. Then we'll have my mother walk by, and see how she's gonna take it, right? You know, like, "Stella, what're you doing here? No! You gotta get away!" You know, how is he gonna tell my mother that he's gonna meet this broad or something, you know? So we made him a pimp, that he gotta pimp my mother off, then he tried to pimp us off . . .

121

Frank and Gail outside the Hotel Van
Rensslaer, NYC, circa 1967

While and he and Gail were living
(none too extravagantly) at the Hotel
Van Rensslaer on Eleventh, sharing
accommodations with a few
cockroaches, Zappa fleshed out the
character of Willie. He added to the

story of Annie and Cynthia by creating Willie as a composite of working Pimps in this area of New York, all so proud of the way they could sell their "floozies" to the buying public...

I'm a little pimp with my hair gassed back
Pair a khaki pants with my shoe shined black
Got a little lady ... walk the street
Tellin' all the boys that she can't be beat
Twenty dollah bill (I can set you straight)
Meet me onna corner boy'n don't be late
Man in a suit with a bow-tie neck
Wanna buy a grunt with a third party check
Standin' onna porch of the Lido Hotel
Floozies in the lobby love the way I sell:

HOT MEAT HOT RATS HOT CATS HOT
RITZ HOT ROOTS HOT SOOTS
HOT MEAT HOT RATS HOT CATS HOT
ZITZ HOT ROOTS HOT SOOTS

The song spoke of doing business with all types to make a buck, which led to the brilliant line, "man in a suit with a bow-tie neck, wanna buy a grunt with a third party check"…you could only imagine Willie's response to that request! But, of course, if there had been an "economic downturn" then perhaps Willie may have taken this form of payment…a pimps gotta do what a pimps gotta do when the market is bad, don't ya know! So through this line we are able to see how Zappa purposefully led the listener to view the song as a reality of trying to stay alive on the mean New York streets of capitalism. Zappa spoke to the way that laissez-faire economics had infiltrated into every aspect of society, turning beautiful, precious living beings into nothing more than just "hot meat…hot rats". The perverse reality of "floozies" in a lobby loving the way that their "pimp" could drum up business…selling their bodies for sexual purposes to a seemingly endless stream of lost souls…all made possible by our incongruous compliance with society…the Matrix.

So, who's to blame??? The big, bad government or the filthy-rich corporations??? Sure, they are the instruments by which our little game of life is manipulated, but clearly the blame lies with ourselves for allowing such horrific realities to exist! What is the self-esteem level of Willie the Pimp, such a "supa-fine" salesman, trafficking in human souls? Huh? Ever thought about such things before? What about the girls who loved the way that Willie sold off pieces of their souls so regularly? And who was that customer "with a bow-tie neck"??? The same gentleman who was playing the role of "Bow-tie Daddy" from the We're Only in it for the Money album? The lecherous, judgmental father and husband who had to interrupt his after-work "marketing" ritual (see copious amounts of alcohol) to drive home (drunk) and deal with his moral-less daughter? Did Bow-tie Daddy first stop off at a certain, Lido Hotel, for a "release"? All of these "coincidences" resulting in this pathetic trifecta of human souls milling about the entrance to a grand cesspool, as the currents of life accidentally and randomly swept them into one another's acquaintances...you know, the bullshit story sold to us as humanity evolving from apes! If someone wants to pick-pocket God from your existence for "Darwinism", then, at the very least, have them prove their "facts". There are absolutely NO PROOFS of any "missing links" in the supposed evolutionary chain of humans evolving from monkeys...NOT ONE! But it gets worse...in addition to this egregious lie that we were once "monkeys", there are NO SIGNS that human beings are evolving at all. In fact, doesn't this song in a very direct manner show just how far humanity has DE-EVOLVED from God's grace? With the help of the status quo and their "friend", modern theoretical science, humans have gone from being God's chosen creations on this stationary plane, at the center of the known universe, to de-evolving RATS feeding off of one another in the great cesspool known as "life in the big city"! And when you view the song from this unique perspective, suddenly it takes on a whole deeper meaning...including all of the "hoopla" that Beefheart put into his vocal (and the reason why Zappa chose Captain Beefheart to be the "official" voice of the album)! Seedy, grimy and greasy human beings who have have fallen from grace into the bowels of modern society! THIS is the true story of Willie the Pimp, and the overall theme from this album...the fantastic duality of the human species...in one moment soaring high upon the winds, while in the next, little rats festering in society's depths! Once again, this song represented Frank Zappa not pulling any punches to let humanity know just exactly where he was coming from.

"MODERN AMERICANS BEHAVE AS IF INTELLIGENCE WERE SOME SORT OF HIDEOUS DEFORMITY."

Frank Zappa

This quote from Frank spoke volumes to his belief in the importance of an Open Mind...closed minded people, who judge before inspection (Einstein, "the height of ignorance") shut off the realm of possibility where miracles are created...

TRACK 3 – SON OF MR. GREEN GENES

"Eat your greens, don't forget your beans and
celery, don't forget to bring your fake I.D. eat
a bunch of these...magnificent...with
sauerkraut...eat a grape, a fig, a crumpet too,
you'll pump 'em right through."
Frank Zappa, from the song, Mr. Green
Genes, off the album, Uncle Meat

129

Side one concluded with a track that was constructed in almost the same manner as Willie the Pimp (both just over nine minutes in length), Son of Mr. Green Genes. Just like "Willie", "Green Genes" had a written, intricate melody section that lasted all of one minute and twenty seconds before Zappa launched into a series of his guitar solos, but this time they were broken up with instrumental breaks featuring the work of Ian Underwood on the Piano, Organ and Saxophone. The tone of the song was much closer to that of Peaches en Regalia, with its bright, celebratory sounds and intricate horn charts. Zappa also deployed his masterful Production/Engineering skills on "Green Genes" as well...as on "Peaches", Zappa recorded the entire rhythm section at "fast" speed; while adding the remaining percussive overdubs in while these basic tracks were being played back at "half" speed. Thus, as on "Peaches", all of the percussive overdubs came off as other-worldly in tone and very unique. They were also instrumental in keeping the song's frantic pace moving forward.

The Son of Mr. Green Genes was an instrumental re-arrangement of the song Mr. Green Genes from the brilliant, Uncle Meat album. This repeated connection with the television character Mr. Green Genes (from the Captain Kangaroo show), along with the choice of "Captain" Beefheart as the album's lone vocalist, led people to speculate that Zappa was somehow related to the character, which was very funny indeed and has grown into a grand "urban legend"! Just like the other two songs on side one, "Green Genes" was also done in 4x4 time and had that tight band sound. Besides Underwood providing his outstanding work on the Piano, Organ, multiple Clarinets and Saxophones, Max Bennett returned on Bass and gave another Funky, wandering bass line that became very Jazzy after the song's principle melody was completed. Behind the kit, Zappa went with the legendary

Jazz Drummer, Paul Humphrey, who provided a much more bouncy, Jazzy beat than that of Guerin's aggressive Rock beat on "Willie". And this is precisely why the song sounds and fits within the style of "Peaches", even though it was written in the same vein as Willie the Pimp.

The legendary Paul Humphrey behind "the kit"

Zappa's series of guitar solos on "Green Genes" didn't have the same tonal intensity to that of "Willie", but they weren't lacking for skill or effect. Zappa played these solos as hybrids of Jazz and Rock and they really delivered in their fluidity (see Jeff Beck) and their ability to seamlessly connect all these guitar runs together through the instrumental breaks! Again, Zappa was powerfully demonstrating to the world just how good of a guitarist and soloist he was…all on his modified Gibson Goldtop…

Zappa's 1952 modified Gibson Goldtop that he used on Hot Rats, auctioned in 2007 for a six-figure sum

Thus, with the Son of Mr. Green Genes, Zappa was able to expand on the album's ingenuity and originality by creating a very tightly constructed Pop song, with Jazz overtones, that somehow extended into a lengthy jam, without managing to resemble Pop, Rock, Jazz or the Blues. This song was truly a hybrid of Zappa and his mind, alone, and it remains to this day as a song that really defies categorization. However, the one unifying theme of the song was excellence...every single performance was sizzling and kept perfect time within this challenging piece of music. Adding to this legend was the song's outro where it seemed that no one wanted the track to end, as Underwood, Zappa and Humphrey continued to add flourish after flourish to what already sounded like the song's ending. Also, Zappa and Underwood concluded their performances with a series of power chords (on the guitar, piano and organ), completing another outstanding song and a truly

legendary, side one, of the album!

"Eat your shoes, don't forget the strings and socks, even eat the box you bought 'em in, you can eat the truck that brought 'em in...garbage truck, mouldy garbage truck...eat the truck and driver and his gloves, nutritiousness, deliciousness, worthlessness"
Frank Zappa, from the song, Mr. Green Genes, off the album, Uncle Meat

TRACK 4 – LITTLE UMBRELLAS

Zappa's "Little Umbrellas"...was Frank
referencing a journey with these?

Side two opened with the very jazzy composition, Little Umbrellas, one of my all-time favorite Zappa songs. It tells the story of a bowl of little umbrellas that live in the Royal Garden Hotel, across the street from the Kensington Market in London...okay, well maybe not. In fact, maybe the song was a journey of sorts for

Frank...using psilocybin mushrooms as the vehicle? This notion might seem a little "far out" for some, so let me explain...from the opening, haunting minor chords played by Ian Underwood on the piano, to his layered alto/soprano sax phrasings, this song was a bizarre combination of the calculated and complex to the surreal and strangely pleasing. In fact, if you close your eyes, clear your mind, and then listen to the song, the music reveals itself as a journey...seriously! Every single time I perform this ritual, Little Umbrellas takes me places...always different and always vivid. And the one time that I listened to "Umbrellas" while on psilocybin, it was so clear, at least to me, that Zappa was definitely "on mushrooms" when he composed this little masterpiece. Now, I am aware of Zappa's personal feelings about "drugs", and his various comments, but there are two key points to mention, (1) Zappa was concerned about anyone needing a drug/crutch to get them through their problems...regardless of whether they were natural substances or not, "drugs" are a distraction away from living in the moment, which should be our only goal in life, and (2) Zappa ripped on weaponized drugs from agencies like the CIA (LSD, Crack, etc.), not natural hallucinogens, he himself admitted to having eight marijuana cigarettes in his life...Frank didn't hate Cannabis, it just didn't do anything for him (other than give him a headache). To that end, I am certain Frank wasn't against anything that grew naturally, and there were a lot "mushrooms" floating around Laurel Canyon in the late Sixties...

God's natural hallucinogens, such as psilocybin mushrooms, are a gateway to a direct connection with Mother Nature and God; however, they are only designed to open this sacred pathway! Once connected, repeating the experience (again and again) puts the focus on the journey, and not the destination...which is God!

To fully understand what I am saying here, you would have to experience psilocybin at least once in your life (and if you haven't, why are you here on this Earth???) Again, let me state that I am not advocating that every human being should constantly experiment with psilocybin, not at all...as Alan Watts said...

"If you get the message, hang up the phone. For psychedelics are simply instruments like microscopes, telescopes and telephones. The biologist does not sit with eye permanently glued to the microscope, he goes away and works on what he has seen."

However, let me also be clear that psilocybin was created by God, and left in abundance for all to happily happen upon (just do a search on Reindeer and Psilocybin Mushrooms). Psilocybin is a perfectly safe, harmless, natural creation that opens the human THIRD EYE (what is known as the Pineal Gland), which is our portal to the non-physical and our "long-distance connection" to God. So, to let Fear, through societal lies, prevent you from experiencing the divine journey of psilocybin would be a terrible loss. As Terence McKenna said,

Perhaps the best presentation that I have ever watched regarding the ABSOLUTE TRUTH about psilocybin was done by the brilliant Bill Hicks (my brother-in-arms)...

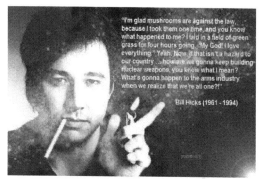

"I'm glad mushrooms are against the law, because I took them one time, and you know what happened to me? I laid in a field of green grass for four hours going, "My God! I love everything." Yeah. Now if that isn't a hazard to our country ...how are we gonna keep building nuclear weapons, you know what I mean? What's gonna happen to the arms industry when we realize that we're all one?!"

Bill Hicks (1961 - 1994)

https://youtu.be/3PJZp5Xd6y8

Musically, the song resembled a journey on psilocybin, especially a first-time experience. The song opened with a very flat note by Max Bennett on his upright bass, which then led into Ian Underwood's irregular, frenetic minor chord piano melody. This was designed by Zappa to give the listener the impression that something weird, unusual and unknown was happening. From there, Zappa created a unified synthesized sound by perfectly combining Underwood's performances on both the alto and soprano saxophones. This sound was other-worldly, a very unique and exotic sonic resonance, so that the listener's suspense about the song's "purpose" was sustained. Also, Underwood's saxophone performance was very lyrical...from the first time I heard this song, I have always (very naturally) attempted to apply some form of lyric/scat to accompany the sax-driven melody. It wasn't until the song broke into its "chorus" melody that Underwood's piano shifted from the slightly uneven, minor chords to a series of gorgeous, classically inspired, piano flourishes...giving the listener the sense of beauty and wonderment. Again, for those who have journeyed on psilocybin, they will understand when I say that this musical progression accurately reflects the first-time experience on these mushrooms. You really aren't quite sure what is happening, things begin to change, the tempo of your former reality is altered, becoming slightly off-kilter, you become aware that your heart rate has elevated in anticipation...all as your ego maintains a healthy dose of worry and concern. Suddenly, the "contrasty" elements of the experience begin to settle down, your heart rate slows, and then you become AWARE of things outside of your five senses. You are now FEELING your reality instead of thinking it. Many people actually experience an extended period of giggling, or laughing hysterically, before they settle into the unending wonderment of the experience.

From there, the song segued into a beautiful Ian Underwood performance on the electric piano...a sound modified to somewhat resemble the harpsichord, hinting at a heavenly, or angelic state. After this solo, the song then contrasted Underwood's beautiful, melodic sounds against his frenetic, principle piano melody. The ensuing moments perfectly reflected the human mind continuing to process this angelic feeling of the psilocybin against our former chaotic reality. The two states-of-mind juxtaposed creating this period of competition within the mind (white noise), instead of us letting go and falling harmlessly into the beauty, peace and tranquility that was waiting (harmony). At the two-minute mark of the song, the harmony won-out, as Underwood proceeded with a gorgeous piano melody that led into his brief and bittersweet solo on the recorder, generating a profound sense of self-discovery, essence, in a rare moment when our psyche is being completely honest with the rest of us. Please note, that through all of this, Underwood's uneven piano melody had disappeared, and was replaced with the more notable presence of both Bennett's warm upright bass and Guerin's gentle and warm cymbal work. Zappa was creating a sense of comfortable benevolence for the listener...and we know that this is the case because after Underwood's touching use of the recorder, the song's returned to its uneven piano melody, but this time it was placed deep in the background, overshadowed by Underwood's saxophone melody. However, gone was the soprano sax within the mix, replaced by a tenor sax, which changed Underwood's sound from other-worldly to WARM and uplifting...precisely the feelings one receives when they finally let go of their ego, and give in to the Godliness of the psilocybin. In fact, as you listen to the sax melody progress towards the song's ending, there is an incredibly beautiful and warm crescendo of sax sounds, where a flugelhorn is added to generate this heightened sense of awareness. I believe it is a flugelhorn, as the resulting sound appears to be a major second lower. On top of this crescendo, Underwood's recorder reappears and takes the song, fittingly, to its abrupt ending. And again, for all those that have experienced psilocybin, this is often how one's journey ends...far too suddenly, leaving our human essence (the sound of the recorder) feeling a little vulnerable as we re-enter into the inhuman Matrix.

There is a world beyond ours, a world that is far away, near, and invisible. And there is where God lives, where the dead live, the spirits and the saints, a world where everything has already happened and everything is known.

The sacred mushroom takes me by the hand and brings me to the world where everything is known.

"The sacred mushroom takes me by the hand and brings me to the world where everything is known." Remember, natural hallucinogens only exist to OPEN THIS SACRED PATHWAY to God; once it's open, you don't need to continually repeat the journey...you now know the way!

Regardless of whether or not you will allow your mind to accept this Jazzy instrumental as Zappa's ode to the Psilocybin Mushroom, it doesn't change the fact that this uniquely odd three-minute Pop song was a moving journey unto itself. The composition was original, lush and extremely dense, and as such, after literally thousands of listens, it still sounds as unique and fresh today as it did the first time I heard it. That is not only a testament to the musicians and composer, but to the producer. Zappa was never given enough credit for his creativity and prowess as a producer of Rock and Roll albums. Little Umbrellas, like Peaches, was a departure from the overall "groove" and structure of the album, yet Zappa was still able to record these tracks in such a way that they fit seamlessly next to the likes of Willie the Pimp and The Gumbo Variations. Much of that was achieved by Zappa slowing down or speeding up certain instruments, like his percussive work and the bass guitar, and running them back through the control panel with tones and nuances that suggested much of the album had been done by a synthesizer…it wasn't…it was Frank experimenting with the existing technology of the day to get the sounds that he wanted! That really was the album's genius…to create and fit well-structured, Jazz-based songs like "Peaches" and "Umbrellas" alongside the four lengthy, Blues-based, Jazz/Rock Fusion improvisations...and then make it all sound as one unified record! A job very well done!

Me, this Halloween, as the Frank Zappa
Zombie...I think my hair was on some little
umbrellas!

TRACK 5 – THE GUMBO VARIATIONS

"My name is Ian Underwood and I am the straight member of the group, (Suzy Creamcheese:) 'Wowie Zowie'. One month ago, I heard the Mothers of Invention at the (Garrick) Theatre. I heard them on two occasions, and on the second occasion I went up to Jim Black and I said, 'I like your music and I would like to come down and play with you'. Two days later I came up to the recording session and Frank Zappa was sitting in the control room. I walked up and said, 'how do you do, my name is Ian Underwood and I like your music and I would like to play with your group'. Frank Zappa says, 'what can you do that is fantastic?', I said, 'I can play Alto Saxophone and Piano'...and he said, 'alright, whip it out'."

The key to understanding how Zappa designed the Gumbo Variations lay in his preamble to the song...

"(Zappa) Take two...(Paul Humphrey) how many bars...(Zappa) uh, why don't you count it off...you three start together on this..."

It's clear from both the words and structure to the song, that Zappa wanted his quartet to create an extended, open jam...and it was just that...an incredible experiment in improvisation. The basis to the track was the quartet of Zappa (rhythm guitar), Max Bennett (electric bass), the supremely rhythmic Paul Humphrey (drums) along with Ian Underwood on the Organus Maximus, sustaining a very funky groove for thirteen minutes (seventeen minutes on Zappa re-mixed version in 1987) so that the soloists could shine...Ian Underwood on Tenor Sax, Don "Sugarcane" Harris on Violin and Zappa on lead guitar as they intuitively layered their improvisations onto the core rhythm section! Ultimately, "Gumbo" was an extended Blues Jam that featured long sections of improvisational Jazz, free-form Jazz, R&B Funk, gritty Rock and Roll, Jazz/Rock Fusion and possibly even the kitchen

153

sink! Even members of the rhythm section got in on the soloing, with both Paul Humphrey and Max Bennett taking turns at driving the song's progression. For both men, playing on this album must have been an absolute blast and a great departure from a lot of their LA session work (e.g. the Partridge Family). Also, by playing on Zappa's fusion record, it opened a lot of doors into the world of Rock and Roll for both men. Humphrey ended up playing with Steely Dan, Michael Franks, Jerry Garcia, Al Kooper and even Marc Bolan (it beat the pants off of playing for Lawrence Welk's TV show). Humphreys connection with Jean Luc-Ponty on this album also led to them working together. For Max Bennett, his work on Hot Rats led him to the likes of Joni Mitchell, Michael Franks, Michael McDonald and George Harrison. Bennett was of course a co-founder of the fabulous LA session group, The L.A. Express, with Zappa co-bandmate, John Guerin...plus,

Bennett re-connected with Zappa on Chunga's Revenge and other assorted sundries. I can guarantee you that both men would have cherished these sessions with Frank, and looked back fondly on their performances from Hot Rats!

But if there was a dominant figure on the Gumbo Variations, it was that master-of-trades, Ian Underwood...his acidic, gritty organ work set the tone for a decade of similar sounds and performances within the Rock and Roll world; but it was his tenor sax performance that truly dominated this song. Underwood gave an impassioned six-plus minute performance that crossed over from Jazz into the avant-garde. It was one of the finest saxophone solos that Underwood ever performed, screeching out note after note in a powerful, very inventive fashion. Underwood started by driving the song's elongated intro into a crescendo of

155

sorts, alongside Zappa's wonderful rhythm guitar part. From there, Underwood settled in and performed stunning saxophone runs one after another for six minutes and twenty seconds! At times his performance was styled as traditional Jazz, while at others, free-form...but Underwood also stepped outside the stylistic boundaries of Jazz, and was completely unconventional and irreverent at times. And I believe throughout the song, he played to please the unconventional ear of one Frank Zappa. Also, Underwood was soloing over a number of stylistic changes to the song itself. Sometimes he played over a laid-back, R&B/Funk groove, while at other times gritty Rock and Roll and even soulful Blues. However, no matter how the song shifted, Underwood's sax solo sounded front and center and right at home.

Ian Underwood "whips it out"

Underwood's brilliant solo segued
seamlessly (another tribute to
Producer, Frank Zappa) into
"Sugarcane" Harris' violin solo.
Zappa grew up as a huge fan of
Harris' performances and

approached Shuggie Otis about getting Harris to perform on the album. Otis found out that "Sugarcane" had been partaking in too many "sweets" and was in prison at the time in California for a drug possession charge...Frank Zappa bailed Harris out of jail so that he could play on the album! In similar fashion to Underwood (which made the song flow along so seamlessly, absent of time), Harris played his violin with great passion pitching, squealing and screeching his sounds throughout the almost five-minute solo. And while not as avant-garde as Underwood's performance, Harris still explored at great range of sounds and went on a number of fluid runs. It was an absolute monster performance by "Sugarcane", as he rewarded Zappa a hundred times over for bailing him out of prison. I've listened to a number of great "Sugarcane" solos over the years, especially live, but I've never heard one better.

Zappa, in studio with his Gibson Goldtop,
rehearsing The Gumbo Variations, 1969

Zappa's guitar work on Gumbo is often overlooked...first, all of his unheralded rhythm guitar work gets passed-over in favor of all the soloing. But it was Zappa's inventive and gritty background guitar parts that really gave Gumbo it's true musical landscape...that of a steamy, swampy sound that really defied any one classification. Second, Zappa's guitar solos were

159

absolutely scintillating, as he built off the solos of both Underwood and "Sugarcane" Harris. The first minute and twenty-second run was so intense and moving, that it naturally picked up the pace and fervor of both Bennett and Humphrey's rhythm section. The diffused sound generated from these extremely fluid runs was created through his wah-wah pedal that was run back through the mixing board. After Zappa the guitarist, completed this first section of his solo, the arranger/producer Zappa then allowed for space to open up in the song so that Paul Humphrey and Max Bennett could take center stage for the next minute. The two men flashed the incredible groove that they had played throughout the song while providing very tasty fills that oozed with Funk! From there, Zappa designed a two-and-a-half minute coda for the ages, where all three soloists played inventively and intensely over one another; and yet, somehow, these three solos (sax,

160

violin and guitar) all seemed to complement one another, rather than to distract. And this is another massive tribute to both Zappa the arranger and Zappa the record producer. The song finally ended with a flourish by Harris on his violin, overtop Ian Underwood's ominous Organus Maximus sound.

The Gumbo Variations
By Frank Zappa

This was such a tremendous song on many, many levels; but mostly because Zappa took a simple R&B rhythm with a basic Funk melody and allowed the "time and space" for superior musicians to create and embellish on top of it! Once again, these musicians fed off of one another to create that "close knit" band feeling from a supposedly "stiff" collection of LA session players. The song also allowed for three great soloists to express themselves, one right after the other, on top of the same Funky beat. It was a musical improvisation at its finest, that once again, somehow, came off sounding like a Rock and Roll band that had played together for a long time…superior musicians, creating superior sounds, under superior conditions!

TRACK 6 – IT MUST BE A CAMEL

The album concluded with the wonderfully odd song, It Must Be a Camel. The song took its title from the shape of the chord sheets...the very unusual melody of this song was highly rhythmic and often made large melodic leaps; thus, these dramatic shapes resembled "humps" when charted...

Musical "camel humps" all across this sheet
of music...

This was certainly a huge departure
from most rock records in 1969
where one or two chords were
typically repeated over and over

165

again, creating a very "static" sound. "Camel" was not a static sounding song, and while most of it was well defined, written out in detail by Zappa, there was a lot of improvisation on this track. Typical with most Jazz records, the musicians always had the flexibility to explore the melody or rhythm when they desired, forcing the other band members to adjust and go with them...this defined a lot of the song! For the previous five songs Zappa had kept the time signature in 4/4, but with "Camel" he went back to normal (for Frank) and altered the time signature.

This intricately arranged song (featuring a lot of wind and keyboard overdubs by Underwood) began with a minute-long percussive intro that featured Zappa on the Piccolo Snare drum providing almost a military styled march against Underwood's change-laden opening piano melody. Zappa played the snare outside of the intro's 4x4 time, adding to the song's time signature confusion. After Zappa led the band through this opening cadenza the song changed to a 6/4 time signature that was littered with dense musical rhythms and a wonderful tenor sax solo by Ian Underwood. Zappa wrote the song similar to a counting exercise for the musicians…certain chords and melody lines sounded to even the most sophisticated listener as very odd time signatures as the musicians often passed over the first note of the bar, but they were always counting the notes carefully to ensure they completed each phrase in whichever time signature they were in. Ian Underwood punctuated the song's principal melody through a series of gorgeous descending triplets on his Tenor sax. Zappa was able to generate that "fat" sound from Underwood's tenor sax by layering in a number of overdubbed sax and clarinet parts, making segments of this song sound like they originated from another reality (which actually explains a lot about Frank)! After Underwood's solo, Zappa jumped into the song's rhythm with his electric guitar adding straight out Rock and Roll riffs and flourishes in a powerful onslaught of sound and energy that was in 4x4 time; this actually caused the band, in particular drummer John Guerin, to misstep the tempo a few times. However, Guerin executed a particularly difficult drum fill as he rhythmically connected the song after Zappa's "solo" from 4x4 time back into the song's principal 6/4 saxophone driven melody…not an easy task at all! The song's coda featured more dissonance and consonance this time between Underwood's sax and Jean-Luc Ponty's Violin fills. This was Ponty's first experience with Zappa, in what would become an excellent "marriage" for them.

Once again, Zappa allowed Underwood's sax work to dominate

"Camel". In between all of his cascading sounds, Underwood played the sax in the style of free-form Jazz with a lot of random notes thrown in that contrasted quite beautifully against the song's lush melody; this interplay between dissonance and consonance was purely sublime and the genius of the song! It is also the reason why this track, and the album in general, are SO IMPORTANT to not only the music world, but to the music listening world as well! Think about this for a moment...how has God constructed EVERYTHING on this Earth and in the sky? One word, DUALITY! For every moment in the light, there is darkness...for every man, there is a woman, for every birth there is a death, for every color, there is another color, for morning, there is night, for abundance there is limitation, for every mountain, there is a valley, for every sun "rise", there is a sunset, for the sun, there is the moon, for every high "tide", there is a low tide, for something heavy, there is something light, for every inhale, there is an exhale...EVERYTHING about our existence is based upon DUALITY, and yet no one ever seems to talk about this, or learn from it. As the closing track to this album, Zappa chose to promote Peace and Equality by creating a song that featured contrast, musically, demonstrating that opposing time signatures could stand together and flow...that discordant and harmonious sounds could, together, create something beautiful and interesting...and that imaginative and odd creations could spark the mind to actually think for itself...and not merely through Pavlovian responses!

THIS is how the brilliant mind of Frank Zappa functioned and these are the thoughts that flowed through his Consciousness. Zappa remains one of the most feared and misunderstood figures of the 20th Century because society WANTS IT

THIS WAY! The eternal presence of fear and doubt in this world (purposefully generated by a tiny group of old, white people hiding behind all the curtains), have become security blankets in which the masses hold themselves together with. Much in the same way that many people wrap themselves up, tightly, in the flags of their nations. We have allowed ourselves to become tiny, frightened, Philadelphia lawyers...harshly judging EVERYTHING that comes across our paths...especially those things that we simply don't understand...like, say, Frank Zappa. Most people that don't "like" Frank's music have NEVER really even listened to it! You may not think that this is a very big deal, but this condition lies at the very heart of ALL OUR PROBLEMS as human beings. We kill the possibility of peace and hope before they even begin through all the grotesque things that we believe in within our minds! Don't fight this truth, go with it...think for a moment...where do virtually ALL of our beliefs come from??? THINK, God-dammit...Parents, Teachers, Politicians, Theoretical Scientists, Religious leaders representing religious institutions, the fucking television set, and from the worst source of garbage of them all...HOLLYWOOD! THESE are the sources of what we all hold dearly as truth in our collective realities! And yet, virtually EVERYTHING that these "sources of information" share with us are LIES...whether purposefully spun, or ignorantly passed on, LIES nonetheless. Thus, we now live in a world where black is white, up is down, mediocrity is the new genius and war means peace...

"What I suspect is, that because Rock and Roll music reaches so many different people, and it does reach them on a repetitive level and it does form an important part of their lives, if you can control that medium you are going to be able to control the ideas which go out to those young people, and there are some

people who don't want to have young people thinking too much because you have to keep them really stupid to buy certain products and to vote for certain people."
Frank Zappa

https://youtu.be/zgVUei2853A

It is only through the understanding of DUALITY that we allow ourselves to truly perceive exactly what Love is and experience our highest possible highs. Without the lowest possible lows achievable in life (a mindless consuming robot going off to war to defend your country against brown people with only rocks to defend themselves), we truly wouldn't be

173

able to conceive of anything except the constant state of Love, losing those incredible moments of what Professor Tolkien described as eucatastrophe (the sudden turn from disaster to victory)...

"I coined the word 'eucatastrophe': the sudden happy turn in a story which pierces you with a joy that brings tears (which I argued it is the highest function of fairy-stories to produce). And I was there led to the view that it produces its peculiar effect because it is a sudden glimpse of Truth, your whole nature chained in material cause and effect, the chain of death, feels a sudden relief as if a major limb out of joint had suddenly snapped back. It perceives – if the story has literary 'truth' on the second plane...that this is indeed how things really do work in the Great World for which our nature is made. And I concluded by saying that the Resurrection was the greatest 'eucatastrophe' possible in the greatest Fairy Story – and produces that essential emotion: Christian joy which produces tears because it is qualitatively so like sorrow, because it comes from those places where Joy and Sorrow are at one, reconciled, as selfishness and altruism are lost in Love."

In other words, God created Duality so that we would come to fully understand what Love, Light and Happiness truly are. All of the corrupt, fascist politicians that roam this Earth, in every country, stealing away our personal liberties through lies, only exist so that we can truly understand what real freedom looks like, and truly is. They don't exist to control us or scare us, they are actors placed into these roles to show us exactly what we DON'T NEED and DON'T WANT! Our only "job" in life is to choose our reality through the decisions we make in every moment! Why do we continue to "democratically" elect our various leaders, through these public shams known as elections, when CLEARLY WE ALL KNOW that these "leaders" are neither democratic nor responsive to our needs??? We should be thanking them, with laughter, for their pathetic roles as we show them the exits from our public circus! Frank Zappa knew that only the individual mind mattered...a free, unencumbered mind that could reason and think for itself...a mind that balanced thinking with feeling...and for this Zappa (and his music) has been censored and shoved to the back of society's closet as some sort of twisted personal pleasure...like so much sex vomited on the pages of dirty magazines!

"Look, I'm not a villain.
I'm an honest person
and I'll say what I believe,
and if that's what it takes
to be a villain,
I'll put on the black cape any day."

-Frank Zappa

EPILOGUE

As an expression of Zappa's true genius, Hot Rats only featured a few non-sequitur lines of lyrics and yet the entire album "spoke" a ton of truth! From the synchronistic nature of Love (Peaches en Regalia), through human slavery caused by our fake monetary and economic systems (Willie the Pimp), to enlightenment of the mind by partaking in God's magical Little Umbrellas, and finally to the personal empowerment of embracing God's dualistic Earth (Son of Mr. Green Genes, the Gumbo Variations and It Must Be a Camel), Zappa created a musical journey of the mind that was both original and thoughtful. There was never a record like Hot Rats before its release, and there hasn't been anything truly like it since. Thus,

there is an eternal gift from Zappa
with this album...in that you can
never tire of its appeal because of its
originality. Plus, it's an album that
EMBRACED stylistic differences,
and brought them together
demonstrating to anyone with an
open mind that if this is possible on a
sonic level, it is very possible at a
human level! On Hot Rats, Zappa
was challenging humanity to awaken
their minds to a free state of
Consciousness, through all of the
albums unique and inventive
processes...

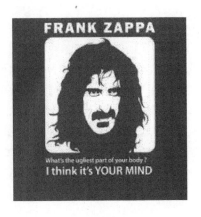

Perhaps the most central theme in all of the books in this series, on the Most Important Rock Albums, is that we have become a DISEASED society; certainly physically, as we have been tricked into ingesting pure toxins...but I am mostly referring to our DISEASED MENTAL state. From the moment we are born, we are PROGRAMMED to believe in an upside down world where Fear dominates the "out there", which is all that exists, and that we must simply do our best to navigate through these waters laced with mines! However, as with all things that originate within society, it is a LIE! The only thing that truly exists is the freedom of the Individual, and that freedom can ONLY BE FOUND BY GOING WITHIN ONESELF. For it is within that our connection to God, and thus ourselves, truly exists!!!

Really the whole album was a precursor to Frank's orchestral works to come, combining a variety of musical styles masterfully into what can only be described as the perfect synthesis for an experiment gone terribly right. Again, as I stated during this album's overview, in the fall of 1969 there hadn't been anything quite like Hot Rats. The album surpassed the emerging attempts at Fusion by Gary Burton, Miles Davis and the band Chicago to create a new sub-genre of Rock and Roll, Jazz/Rock Fusion. The mix on the album between Jazz, the Blues, Funk, R&B and Rock and Roll was seamless, as this collection of principally Bluesy songs, constructed like Jazz compositions, came out as if they were played by a Rock band that had been together for some time! After Miles Davis' 1970 album, Bitches Brew and Traffic's 1971 album, The Low Spark of High Heeled Boys, more and more bands from both sides of the musical spectrum began to incorporate elements of Fusion into their albums. But it wasn't until the Seventies that bands like Weather Report and Steely Dan matched the genius and integrity that Zappa created with Hot Rats! Again, Hot Rats didn't come off as a Jazz record performed by a pioneering Rock artist, it was a Rock and Roll record that featured a lot of various elements that seemed to include Jazz. And I used the word "seemed" purposefully because in one moment "Jazz" was front and center on the album, but then magically, in the next moment it was gone...and in that analysis lies the true genius of the record. Zappa applied nature's duality to the construct of these songs. He purposefully took divergent musical themes and tones and placed them on top of one another to demonstrate just how melodic and harmonious these disparate elements could be together...this is the essence musically to Hot Rats.

The album was also perfectly arranged and produced by Zappa, using brand new, state-of-the-art equipment to achieve what he was looking for in terms of the album's sonics...and how he made all these sounds blend seamlessly together into what resembled a Rock and Roll performance...thereby creating Fusion! The album was also

181

legendary for its Bass guitar sounds and its clarity; the cleanliness of this record's sound for 1969 was almost unthinkable, which is likely another reason why the album continues to be topical and not dated. A lot of international attention fell upon Ian Underwood after Hot Rats was released and rightfully so; besides his technical prowess, Underwood developed a Saxophone style on this album that was about exploration and discovery. His sections of free-form Jazz allowed him to randomly go in any direction musically and discover what was "there", which also just happens to be the perfect metaphor for Life! This work brought Underwood to the attention of Jazz titans Lalo Schifrin, Alphonse Mouzon and Gabor Szabo to name just a few!

Frank Zappa memorialized all over Europe with frescos and murals

Zappa became a revelation for so many people around the world (many who were locked behind the Iron Curtain in Eastern Europe) who felt alone and misunderstood with their beliefs. In a bold, confident and powerful manner, Zappa expressed what millions of disconnected people were feeling inside themselves, giving them the confidence to KNOW that how they felt and what they were trying to do in their lives was "okay", that it was to be applauded and celebrated, not shunned as some kind of movement of misfits. He was a hero to all those FREAKS who didn't seem to fit in on any level, because they didn't want to fit in on any existing "levels"…they didn't want to be a part of a plastic, phony society playing the game of money, filled with lies designed to make us conform! Zappa spoke the truth about our human existence and revealed the rigged game that was going on all around us. But he did much more than that…Zappa also demonstrated to these millions of Freaks worldwide how to go about their lives…how to express themselves within society. This gave millions of people hope and purpose that their lives could have real meaning and value, which was a gift that couldn't ever be forgotten or "repaid". And finally, Hot Rats was teaching us to embrace differences, to fuse them together, and never to shun them out of fear...he was teaching us about the Earth's nature of Duality...where darkness isn't to be feared, it is to be thanked for helping us to fully understand and appreciate the light!

Frank Zappa is a major reason why I found the courage to live my life in an authentic, truthful manner, that truly reflected the desires deep inside of me; and why I now live my life outside of the parameters set by society, in a state of perpetual happiness and adventure! Albums like Freak Out!, Absolutely Free, We're Only In It For the Money and Hot Rats were so OUTRAGEOUS, so outside of the box, that they gave me the fearlessness to express myself very differently, especially within high school, of which I attended as little as possible…the results in my life were staggering…the people I met, the books, albums and works of art that crossed my path were life-changing! These Zappa albums led me directly to the writings of Edgar Allan Poe; a creator of worlds that challenged personal beliefs and pushed boundaries like Zappa's records. These works encouraged me to look deep within myself for my own answers and changes; not "out there" in a society that was filled with the lies of the status quo! There simply aren't words to adequately describe how much Frank Zappa (and all of his works) continue to mean to me, and how bold and beautiful this album is…Hot Rats is one of the most important albums ever recorded on a number of levels, and certainly one of the finest as well!

"Politics is the entertainment branch of Industry (Fascism), they do more to entertain us then to serve us…it seems that the problem with government as an institution is it's uniformly bad worldwide, it may be the only thing that binds all nations together is the incompetence of all their governments."

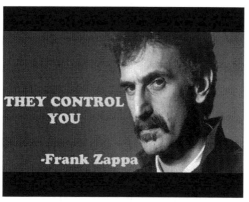

THEY CONTROL YOU

-Frank Zappa

https://youtu.be/a1EqN2mV2TU

"After the murder of Martin Luther King, then you get the Bobby Kennedy assassination and it starts to look like a trend...I mean anybody who thinks these were isolated incidents, isolated "crackpots", I see a trend, I see a mysterious hand behind all of this...the idea, that the possibility that certain types of conspiracies have existed in American politics, because they have existed before allow you to project that could continue to exist to this day...the unions are the mafia, which is the CIA, which is the Catholic Church, which is the government...what's the difference? It's corrupt, it's the same guys pulling the strings!"